Be More, Stress -Less

Realize your best life by re-thinking stress

The Workbook

Jeanne Ricks, CHC

NuDay **N**D**P** Perspectives
Chicago ◈ New York

Cover Art: Jeanne Ricks
Cover Photo: Regina Fleming
Illustrations: Ayanna Johnson
Barbara Haeger illustration on Page 102
Printed in the U.S.A

NuDay **NDP** Perspectives
Chicago ◈ New York

Library of Congress Cataloging-in-Publication Data
Be More, Stress-Less – The Workbook
Pages cm
Includes bibliographical references and index.
ISBN-13: 978-0988527409 (Nu Day Perspectives)
ISBN-10: 0988527405
(e-book)
1. Stress management 2. Respiration 3. Exercise 4/ Self-care.
Health 1. Title

NOTE:

Neither the publisher nor the author is engaged in rendering professional advice or services to the individual reader. The information provided in this book, by necessity is of a general nature and not a substitute for an evaluation or treatment by a competent medical specialist. It is sold with the understanding that the author and the publisher are not engaged in medical, psychological, legal, accounting or other professional services. The dietary & supplemental suggestions are based on tradition, scientific theories or limited research.

While every attempt has been made to provide accurate information, neither the author nor the publishers can be held accountable for any omission or error. Neither the author nor the publisher shall be liable or responsible for any loss or damage allegedly arising from information or suggestion in this book. The author and the publisher specifically disclaim any liability that is incurred from the use or the application of the contents of this book. This information is provided for general educational purposes only and is not intended to constitute (i) medical advice or counseling, (ii) the practice of medicine including psychiatry, psychology, psychotherapy or the provision of health care diagnosis or treatment, (iii) the creation of a physician patient or clinical relationship, or (iv) an endorsement, recommendation or sponsorship of any third party product or service by the author or the author's affiliates, agents, employees, consultants or service providers.

If you have or suspect that you have a medical problem, contact your health care provider immediately.

Appreciations

I would like to thank my family of friends who constantly amaze me with their support and love.

Thank you to my teachers along the way: Many colleagues and friends directly and indirectly helped in the writing of this book ~ my Uncle Percy E. Ricks, Jill Clarke, Bill Weinberg, Jeanne Fletcher Mallette, Johnny (Ananda) Norman, Ruth Anderson, Lisa Fischer, Edna Williams, Delia McVoy, Charles Walton, Kim Walton, Thomas C. Washington, Pamela Nunes, Evette Murray, Paris Eley, Richard P. Stone, Paul Arnold, Frances Connor, Dorette Brown, Miguel Broom, Mark Brooks, Ehryck Gilmore, Paulette de Suzia, Robert Irving III, Edgar Maldonado, Chan, Veronica & Victoria Johnson, Studs Terkel, Joseph Campbell, Howard Thurman, Linus Pauling, Bruce Lipton, Candace Pert, Debbie Ford, Deepak Chopra, Joseph Mercola, Babette Rothschild, Larry Dossey, Brian Weiss, Panache Desai, Rupert Sheldrake, Gary Robert Buchanan, Roger K. Pitman, Ann Albers, Edwina Kee, Jacqueline de Vries, Sheryl Levanthal, Sandy Beltramini, Sharon Mackey-McGee, Karen Witherspoon, Keith Collins, Denise Richardson, Bob McCarthy; Neville Gupta, Mary Ann Donoghue, Christian Villalba, Ella Britton Gibson, Terri Rossi and many others too numerous to name here, but whom I hope know that I am grateful for their friendship and support.

Last but not least, my thanks to you the readers around the world who make all of our efforts worthwhile.

Table of Contents

*I*ntroduction

A workbook? Well really it's more of a play and relax book. This is a tool for any and all who want to take a pro-active position when it comes to stress and its effects on their health and well-being. While the original book 'The Biology of Beating Stress' gives you valuable insight into what happens with your body's physical challenges as well as, your mental and emotional challenges with stress; this workbook was created as a means for delving right in and making immediate changes to restore, recover or create a more balanced, healthy, creative and satisfying environment ~ in home, work or play.

We, as a society have forgotten how to simply 'Be'. The goal here is for you to come away with new awareness of how deep the effects of stress are on your health, and give you immediate ways which you can use to start relieving some of your daily pressures.

This one step will go tremendous lengths towards improving overall health. We take our stress levels for granted ~ it's literally making us sick ~ If everyone would treat themselves and their bodies with just a little more care and kindness we would see leaps in health improvement spanning across all groups. There are small simple things like deep breathing ~ that can make a world of difference!

Let the numbers do a little talking...

*S*tress Statistics

Research Date: 4.6.2012 ~ Verification Source:
American Psychological Association, American Institute of Stress, NY

Top Causes of Stress in the U.S.

	Cause	Factors
1	**Job Pressure**	Bosses, Work Overload, Co-Worker Tension
2	**Money**	Loss of Job, Reduced Retirement, Medical Expenses
3	**Health**	Health Crisis, Terminal or Chronic Illness
4	**Relationships**	Divorce, Death of Spouse, Arguments with Friends, Loneliness
5	**Poor Nutrition**	Inadequate Nutrition, Caffeine, Processed Foods, Refined Sugars
6	**Media Overload**	Internet, eMail, Social Networking, Television, Radio,
7	**Sleep Deprivation**	Inability to release adrenaline and other stress hormones

U.S Stress Statistics	Data
Percent of people who regularly experience physical symptoms caused by stress	77 %
Regularly experience psychological symptoms caused by stress	73 %
Feel they are living with extreme stress	33 %
Feel their stress has increased over the past five years	48 %
Cited money and work as the leading cause of their stress	76 %
Reported lying awake at night due to stress	48 %
Stress Impact Statistics	
Negative impact on personal and professional life	48 %
Employed adults who say they have difficulty managing work and family responsibilities.	31 %
Percent who cited jobs interfering with their family or personal time as a significant source of stress.	35 %
Stress has caused them to fight with people close to them	54 %
Alienation from a friend or family member because of stress	26 %
Percent who say they are "always" or "often" under stress at work	30%
Annual costs to employers in stress related health care and missed work.	$300 Billion
Physical symptoms included	
Fatigue	51 %
Headache	44 %
Upset stomach	34 %
Muscle tension	30 %
Change in appetite	23 %
Teeth grinding	17 %
Change in sex drive	15 %
Feeling dizzy	13 %
Those who cited psychological symptoms experienced the following	
Irritability or anger	50 %
Feeling nervous	45 %
Lack of energy	45 %
Feeling as though you could cry	35 %

4

*S*tress overwhelms your nervous system and floods your body with chemicals to prepare you for "fight or flight". This same emergency response system was designed to save your life in crisis situations ~ where you need to act quickly. Remember ~ your brain hasn't reached a point where it has a state of being called 'just stress'. It only knows crisis or non-crisis ~ *there is no in-between.*

So what you consider "stress" gets re-interpreted by your brain as life-threatening danger! Constant activation simply wears your body down when it's over-stimulated by the stresses of your everyday life. *Why does this affect health?*

You see, in times of stress, without realizing it you're actually bathing yourself in a whole soup of nerve chemicals and hormones like CRH (corticotropin-releasing hormone) and eventually your adrenal glands release another important hormone called cortisol.a powerful anti-inflammatory. (You might be familiar with Cortisone, which is just the drug form of this natural hormone cortisol.) It's as if your body is giving itself multiple shots of that anti-inflammatory hormone. But, *guess what?*

As it continues to do this over-time it dials down your immune system's ability to do its job to fight real infections,

In fact, that cortisol release creates what I call the

Stress Domino Effect

All available resources are switched over to increase your energy level towards fast movement – because it's assumed that you're about to sprint-off full steam away from some life-threatening danger and your brain wants you to have every ounce of strength it can muster for this mad dash to safety.

1. It minimizes energy that was being directed towards your digestion (after all you aren't going to have time for fine dining while on-the-run).

2. It reduces your carbohydrate, protein and fat metabolism, fluid and electrolyte balance.

3. It constricts the pupils of your eyes to help you be able to focus on your attacker.

4. It lowers your immunity and inflammatory responses.

5. It skims-off some of you muscle tissue to produce more glucose for energy.

6. Triglycerides get mobilized from your fat tissues.

7. You have reduced sensitivity to pain; your skin temperature changes.

8. It even turns-off your sex drive (no time for making whoopee).

9. And the little guys in the boiler room are working overtime to pump-up your cardiovascular function speeding-up the heart and contracting blood vessels increasing your blood pressure.

10. Even your lungs are affected as alterations are made in the resistance to airflow in and out (by changing the diameter of the branches of the bronchial tree).

11. Meanwhile, it calculates your potential need for quick burning energy to get you going (glucose and triglycerides were already consumed by your cells in preparation for activity) ~
so that sudden craving you had to munch on something sweet or fatty, *was not random* – it was actually your brain nudging you to provide it with additional kindling for this fire it's building-up.

Whew! A lot happens very quickly when you're under stress.
Imagine ~ all of this is taking place while you're just stressed out sitting in traffic, talking on the phone with customer service, getting new instructions from your boss, talking to your kid's teacher...
You get the picture ~ many little things that happen in your daily life begin to add up and can affect your health quite seriously.

Your doctor will no doubt tell you about even more issues that the stress cortisol response can cause, and confirm for you quite readily that, over-time, if left un-checked ~ stress can be deadly.

This workbook will focus on tools and techniques to enhance what's called 'The Relaxation Response'[10] which puts the brakes on this heightened state of alert and brings your body and mind back into a state of equilibrium. In fact, there are several different techniques offered here which will help you bring your nervous system back into balance by producing the relaxation response.

You're probably thinking "I already know how to relax; I simply don't do enough of it." But truly, the Relaxation Response is more than just lying around on your couch or sleeping-in occasionally. It involves a mentally active process that leaves your body relaxed, calm and focused.

You'll find that learning the basics of these relaxation techniques isn't difficult, but it will take a bit of practice. Research by most stress experts concluded that setting aside at least 10 to 20 minutes a day for relaxation practice is necessary. However, if you'd like to get even more stress relief, you should aim for 30 minutes to an hour.

Does that sound like a huge commitment? Please consider that I've specifically collected many techniques which can be easily incorporated into your existing daily routine ~ practiced at your desk, over lunch or on the bus during your commute.

The best way to start and to maintain your stress reduction practice is to incorporate it into your daily schedule ~ between work, family, school and other commitments.

This is time that you set aside ~ *for you*, and it can enhance all other parts of your life. *Let's get started!*

Getting Started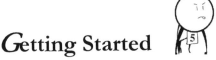

At the core of nearly all stress is the fear and anxiety caused by loss (or potential loss) of what you perceive as 'control'. That's right. Somehow, someway your boundaries have been pushed, your confidence shaken ~ something's out of control ~ your control.

We all try to protect ourselves by attempting to correctly predict and manage the future ~ which we do about as precisely as a five-day weather forecast. Some people act as if they have some sort of moral duty to constantly worry about bad things which might happen to themselves or others about whom they care. There are stress 'carriers' and stress 'bringers' ~ those folks who stress out everyone around them ~ while they just watch the fall-out.

Then there're some needs we carried over from youth that can find us seeking approval from others in myriad ways ~ another useless and potentially hazardous path that can leave you feeling like a pinball being flipped and bounced across the playfield board.

All stress can't be labeled as 'Bad'. Let's face it; some stress is absolutely necessary and appropriate. If early man had not kept alert and appropriately fearful of Saber-tooth tigers, we would not be here to stress over food prices. Perception is key (and whether or not the stress is continual). Small amounts of stress can serve to get you motivated; keep the 'juices flowing.'

The major point is learning to monitor how you perceive the stress in your environment ~ reduce its ability to affect you negatively and then find ways to use the stress energy in a positive beneficial way.

Most of us haven't really considered the way in which we approach our stress. In fact, most of us still deal with stress the same way we did when it was first introduced into our lives as children. Your first lessons in stress were learned right there on the playground, standing in lines at school, in the classroom dealing with teachers and homework demands, dealing with your parents and siblings, etc. *It's time for an update!*

Let's start a fresh approach. We're going to begin by getting control over the one thing that you really do have power over ~ *YOU!*

7 numbers you MUST discuss with your doctor

1. Your **C-Reactive Protein Level** - used to gauge inflammatory activity inside your blood vessels. The Nov. 14, 2002, *New England Journal of Medicine,* concluded that CRP <u>outperforms</u> LDL cholesterol as a predictor of cardiovascular risk.[1] The test costs a whopping $12-$16, and takes only a small amount of blood. In fact, the same blood sample could be sent to a lab for both your cholesterol and C-reactive protein testing.

2. **NMR Lipoprofile Test**, because traditional cholesterol testing is extremely flawed. Research has shown that only about 50% of those who have heart attacks have high LDL.

But, there have been advancements in testing and now the most important test you can get to determine your heart disease risk is the NMR Lipoprofile, which measures your LDL particle number. This test also seeks other markers that can help determine if you insulin resistance, making it even more useful.

What's the test looking for? If you have insulin or leptin resistance, your results will show an increase in LDL particle number and in particular the number of small LDL particles. This NMR Lipoprofile test will measure that particle number too. It will give you an independent score called the lipoprotein insulin resistance score or LP–IR. If your results show that your LP–IR is above the recommended reference range, then chances are that you have leptin and insulin resistance.

You'll find the test easy to get and all major labs offer it. Most insurance policies cover it as well.

3. Your **fasting insulin level:** This means simply where your insulin level is when you haven't eaten for a specific length of time. When you eat, (especially any meal or snack that's high in carbohydrates like fructose or refined grains) this will generate a very quick rise in your blood glucose. Now your body will kick-in. It will boost insulin to compensate for this rise in your blood sugar. This means that when you eat too many carbs, the insulin your body actually releases and promotes fat. It also makes it more difficult for your body to shed the excess weight, as well as excess fat (especially right around your mid-section). This excess insulin is also one of the major contributors to heart disease.

Food is fuel; skip a meal and you'll feel tired and cranky. When you go too long without eating, your blood sugar sinks and mood swings follow. Always strive to eat 4 or 5 small meals spread out through your day, (instead of the standard 2 or 3 larger meals). This will assist your body in maintaining optimal blood sugar levels reducing the risk for serious diet-related chronic diseases, including type-2 Diabetes. This will also cut down your cravings for the less healthy choices because your body is so well fed - *there's no room left for junk!* This single action can greatly reduce your everyday stress levels, by reducing or eliminating the subliminal stress brought on through low energy levels, sense of deprivation and your body's urgency for missing nutrients needed to function properly.

4.   Your **fasting blood sugar level**: Again, just where your blood sugar level is when you haven't eaten for a specific period of time. The number to watch here is a fasting blood sugar level of 100-125 mg/dl because studies have shown that people in this range had a nearly 300 percent increase higher risk of having coronary heart disease than people with a level below 79 mg/dl

5.   Your **HDL/total cholesterol ratio:** HDL percentage is still a handy number to have as a heart disease risk factor. Just how do you get this ratio? Divide your HDL level by your total cholesterol. By the way, ideally this percentage should be above 24 percent. Any number below 10 percent, is a significant indicator of risk for heart disease

6.   Your **triglyceride/HDL ratios**: Reportedly, this percentage should be below 2, so you need to check this with your doctor..

7.   Your **waist circumference**: They call the type of fat that collects around your internal organs, Visceral fat and it's a well-recognized risk factor for heart disease. To evaluate your risk here, the easiest way is by simply measuring your waist circumference.

Who Are You?

Yeah *You!* Every day, every moment of every day, every word spoken, the genesis of every thought and action is invisibly guided by agreements which you have made with yourself ~ most of them unconsciously ~ sometimes based on a religious or family code, or things you've picked-up through your community (neighbors, school, work, friends). There are lines that you've drawn over time. Things which you've told yourself are non-negotiable ~ 'must haves'. Other lines that you've drawn are those which must never be crossed (either by you or anyone else).

These lines are always there ~ whether you're consciously aware or not. They direct your decisions, the way you see others, the way that you conduct yourself in all aspects of your life. They define who you are. These are your Guiding Principles or Core Values.

> *So shouldn't you know what they are ~*
> *be able to speak them out loud?*

This is SO important. Take the time for your _self_ to explore ~ what is really essential to your time on this little blue planet. For your space and your expression of energy in this life ~ what's driving you?

What has this got to do with STRESS?? Perspective.

Once you see the larger picture aspects of 'What Makes You Tick' ~ all the little stuff can be put in its place. You'll be able to define for yourself *why* something going-on in your life lifts you up and why other things are dragging you down. Some things you'll understand immediately are right in-line with your personal guiding principles ~ while others are way out-of-bounds. All improvement in your life begins with clarifying your true core values and then committing yourself to live consistently with them ~ *NOW*.

Quite simply, when you ignore a core value, you'll know it. The signs will be an experience of negative feelings, just not 'motivated', a loss of energy, a general feeling of discontentment or being "out of sorts" and potentially inappropriate anger may pop-up ~ all working against you. This can all happen subliminally if you have never bothered to figure out what your core values actually are.

The contrast comes when you're doing things within that 'sweet spot' of your personal guiding principles ~ things will come more effortlessly, your energy is there; you don't drag yourself around to get things done. You'll more easily identify choices and opportunities which keep you moving forward.
So how do you figure out what they are?

Step One

Lao-tzu is credited for saying, 'The journey of a thousand miles starts with a single step' ~ Well, this is yours. List some one word values that resonate as absolutely crucial to your life. The word 'resonate' is being used to convey that the word you choose should really ring true as an imperative to you from the tip of your toes to the top of your head. [ex. Justice; Freedom; Integrity; Honesty; Respect; Peace; Excellence; Education; Family; Responsibility; Leadership]

No pressure - there are absolutely no "right" or "wrong" answers. As mentioned earlier, things within your life will just *feel* right when you recognize and honor your core values, but will always feel a little "off" if you choose to ignore your guiding principles. So, what matters in your life?

My Guiding Principles

Walking Out Your Door

Keys – *check*. Wallet – *check*. Phone – *check*. Destination – *unknown...?*

Consider for a moment ~ Would you rush out of your front door without knowing where you were headed? A simple enough question - so simple that you're already suspicious of a deeper meaning in it *aren't you?*

Recognize that so many people around you have not got the first clue as to where they're headed. No clue. There's a kind of mindless fog that can easily lull any of us. There are so many things which call upon our attention at any given moment. When we finally *do* have a moment's peace ~ we're too exhausted and stressed-out to even think about ~ thinking.

Sure, having your goals in your head are one thing, but writing them out on paper allows you to organize them and more easily set a real plan into motion to bring your goals to fruition. It forces you to recognize what steps might be necessary, what resources you'll need and to identify what is *or is not* working in your life to reach your desired goal. Sound good?

Setting Goals you'll discover is such a fundamental to finding your way through a life which is often chaotic and time challenged. You spend so much time just putting out one fire after the other. Goals can actually help you feel a little more in control as you witness each brick that you lay on your foundation take you just a little closer. We all need to feel as though we're getting somewhere and not just riding in a runaway car. This helps put you in the driver's seat, with an accurate GPS and nice clean windshield.

Your goal can relate to your personal life, career, health, family, business. It can be related to any aspect of your life that you can think of.

The clearer you are about what you want, the more likely you are to do more and more of the things that are consistent with achieving them. Meanwhile, you'll do less and less of the things that don't help to get the things you *really* want for your life.

1. Define *why* your goal is important to you. Be honest. Make sure that your goal aligns with your personal guiding

principles, skills, talents and dreams. Setting a goal and pursuing it without knowing why the heck you want it is a sure-fire way of stopping short of your goal.

Here's a secret ~ at the core of any goal that you make, will be a basic desire for more peace, joy or love. Yes, I know this all sounds very 'Hippie 60's or 80's 'New Age' but, hear me out. For any goal ask yourself the single question 'What will this bring me once I have it?" and as you go down layer after layer you will find that ultimately, your true goal is for more peace, love or joy.

Examples:
New car = easier transport without worry of costly repairs or more space for kids = peace & joy.

Better job = lees worry financially = peace & joy [AND even = more free time = more quality time with partner = love]

For this reason it is very, very, very important NOT to base the reason for your goal on some of what we term as negative emotions: i.e. Anger, Sadness, Fear, Guilt, etc.

Why? Because first of all just planting your seeds in what might be called 'bitter earth' is just never a good starting place is it? Regardless of your spiritual foundation consider this ~ any gain you make from this negative space will reduce it in one of your other core values ` love, peace of mind or joy'. Let's use an example of 'revenge' being your goal. Any 'joy' you think you may have derived from that act will completely reduce your satisfaction in the areas of peace and love ~ without question.

Mitigation: Keep your goals self-directed. Drive in your own lane.

2. Moment of Truth. Ok, you'll need to pause a moment and candidly, in a non-judgmental way, consider any beliefs that you hold about _yourself_ which conflict with the actualization of your goals. This is a biggie because it is just these self-limiting views that will keep you running in place. If there is any doubt in your mind that you may not be able to achieve something, then you can't give it your all. You know the kind of thoughts I'm talking about:

I don't have enough money to pursue this. I can't afford it.

I can't do _____.

I don't have educational background; maybe I'll do it after I've gained _____degree.

There are others so much more deserving.

I have bad luck.

I just don't have any time.

I don't have the right connections.

I will try but, will probably fail.

I have to wait until the kids are out of college.

I tried _____ and that didn't work, so why should this?

Sound familiar? It's so easy ~ too easy to get caught-up in old patterns and artifacts from your past. Remember, the biggest job of your unconscious is to keep you 'safe', and consequently to instill fear in you *not* to pursue goals outside of your comfort zone. This is 100% natural and instinctive. We all wrestle with it.

But, just because you have a negative or self-limiting thought, doesn't mean that it's actually ***true***!

Put them into a list and address each one independently with more constructive and supportive views ~ like those wise, wonderful things you would say if you were just talking with a good friend.

Start simply by evaluating whether your self-criticism or limiting belief really is true. So many of our so-called 'self' judgments and limitations have leaked-in overtime from many sources (family, siblings, teachers, friends, media). We're on auto-pilot most of the time by nature, so we don't notice that we've even collected them. Honestly, we take more care in selecting our flavor of toothpaste than we do in selecting our thoughts. We just let old thought loops play away, snatching our attention this way and that, without the slightest consideration of where all that junk came from. You CAN select your thoughts! Don't simply accept them as true because you hear them playing repetitively inside your head! There's a lot of untrue stuff playing around in your un-conscious mind ~ old commercial slogans, song lyrics, shopping lists; comments made by teachers, parents…junk!

Secondly, if it's something that you do believe to be genuinely true, then take a moment to determine also whether it's 100% accurate. Really?

What percentage would you really assign to it?

Is it less accurate now than it was in your past?

Have you made improvements over time?

Do you have other ways to work around it, support or even eliminate it?

3. Focus on goals that are obtainable and then set yourself smaller short-term goals that lead-up to your long-term goal. Short term goals are ones which can be achieved in 1-6 months. Medium term goals can be achieved in 7-11 months. Long term goals might take 1 year - 5 years.

Your goal should be in some way measurable as well. So create specific targets along your 'road of attainment.' With this yardstick you're more likely to stay on track and reach certain milestones to give yourself that boost and confidence to keep moving forward.

4. Write it out clearly and in as much detail as you can. *Why?* A vague goal can lead to procrastination since you may not be sure exactly how to get started with your goal. Be specific. Really, the more you write and rewrite your goals ~ *and* the more you think about them, the clearer you will become about them.

Clarity is what we so often lack. Be clear.

5. Research and empower yourself with all of the information that you can find. Take a look into other successful people who have already reached similar goals and make note of the road that they took to get there. *Why re-invent the wheel?*

6. List everything that you'll need to attain your goal. This includes, making note of any assets or resources which you *already* have that will assist you in easily reaching your goal.

7. Organize the items on your list into a plan by placing them in the proper order and priority. As you think of new items, just add them to your list.

   Note: If this involves enlisting the aid of others, be very, <u>*very*</u> careful in selecting only those who you know will support and encourage you in positive ways. Unfortunately, there are people who may not always have our best interests at heart.

8. Candidly review and analyze your current position, your start point ~ now.

9. Set a reasonable deadline for yourself. If it is a large goal, then break it down into sub-deadlines and write them down in order of importance.

10. Make your plan and put it into motion. Do something towards it immediately! *Now!*

11. Do something <u>every</u> <u>single</u> <u>day</u> that moves you toward one or more of your goals.

12. Review your goals *daily. Why?* For the same reason you keep your hands on the steering wheel when driving. When you review them consider whether your goals may have shifted. You will find yourself deleting goals that are no longer as important as you once thought ~ and find other things taking their place.

13. *Be Flexible!* Do not become so fixated on one goal that you step over other opportunities on the way. What you sometimes perceive as an obstacle may very well lead you to a creative alternative which becomes an opening for something new

    "Our destiny is frequently met in the very paths we take to avoid it." (quote generally attributed to Jean de La Fontaine)

14. Everyday take out a few moments, close your eyes and just see yourself at the completion of your goal. Here you want to literally see it, feel it, taste it, etc. make it real ~ use the very powerful tool of your mind to literally 'BE' in the moment you achieve your goal and enjoy your feelings.

*S*uggestions for More 'Activated' Goal Writing:

☞ Begin with just a very simple sentence that states your intention.

☞ Write it in present tense and use the word 'I'.

☞ Now, take your sentence and write it on several 'sticky notes'.

☞ Place them in your car, on your monitor, on your bathroom mirror and by your bed.

☞ Before shutting your eyes at night, read your sentence a few times. Then spend 1-2 minutes visualizing what achieving it will actually feel like (deep in your gut). See the actual details of it.

And here's another biggie ~ feel deep, deep gratitude for it having already happened.

That simple little sentence will gain more and more power as you imprint it on your unconscious.

The more you work with your goals ~ daily honing, refining, nourishing them through positive action ~ the more results you will see. AS you begin to see even small results~ you gain more confidence. AS you gain more confidence you exude this in every aspect of your life and you become a more positively motivating being. AS you become more positive ~ you attract more and more of that energy to you~ more like-minded people, situations and opportunities. This isn't magic, though it may begin to feel that way. Enjoy the ride!

*L*imits, Left-overs
– the Stuff I'm *Leaving Behind Now!*

Limitation	Truth%	Potential 4 Change%	Solutions & Workarounds

22

*M*y Goals

Affirmed Goal	Skills Required	Resources	Tasks for Completion	Notes

Now let's hone it down further & make it all more manageable! We'll reduce it into Monthly, Weekly & Daily tasks that move you closer to your goal.

This simple self-monitoring tool works for 3 simple reasons, it.....
- Helps you document and keep track of your progress.
- Assists you in identifying what is working and what is not.
- Helps you to think about your goals and what steps you will have to take to achieve them

Listing reason(s) why any particular goal is important to you helps you stay connected and inspired. Simple reminders give you a renewed jolt of enthusiasm and purpose each time you write it.

You don't want to set yourself up with 'negative forecasting' *but*...you *definitely* want the ability to anticipate potential realistic challenges. Listing potential challenges allows you to think about these possibilities while you're not already under pressure, which will allow you the space to create positive solutions before the problem even arises. This way you are ready if you need to be.

This said, there is a fine line to be cautious of between positive preparation for potential challenges and plain old-fashioned worrying. You must be vigilant to distinguish the difference. If you've identified a weak spot in your plans or goals, have considered workable solutions and then moved forward ~ great! If you still walk around thinking about it constantly, you're obsessing and you're in constant low-level stress ~ the very thing we're working towards reducing by focusing your energy on your goals.

If you still have that little niggling voice in the back of your head ~ that 'Doubting Thomas', that anxiety ~ ask yourself:

What's the probability that the challenge to your goal will really present itself? 50%? 20%?

How prepared are you in terms of the solutions that you've come-up with? 90%? 75%?

When you're concerned about a negative outcome to any would-be problem scenario, consider what's within your power to prevent that outcome ~ write it out or do it if it requires action; and then let go of those worrisome thoughts. "Worry is nothing less than the misuse of your imagination." (Ed Foreman)

You'll soon see how much less stressful achieving your goals is with these simple tools!

<u>M</u>y Monthly Goal Confirmation:
Date_____

Goal(s) to work towards this month:

Reason or Importance of the goal(s) to me:

Any potential obstacles which might be encountered in pursuit of my goal(s) this month:

Power Plays to address these little setbacks:
   1.
   2.
   3.
   4.

Week	Goal(s)	Tasks	Notes
1			
2			
3			
4			

<u>_M_y Weekly Goal Confirmation:</u>

Date_____

Goal(s) to work towards this week:

Reason or Importance of the goal(s) to me:

Any potential obstacles which might be encountered in pursuit ofmy goal(s) this week:

Power Plays to address any little setback:
    1.
    2.
    3.
    4.

Day	Goal(s)	Tasks	Notes
Sunday			
Monday			
Tuesday			
Wednesday			
Thursday			
Friday			
Saturday			

*M*y Goal View for the Day:
Date_____

Goal(s)	Tasks	Notes

*B*ig Picture Goals

*O*k, now that you've settled-in to the concept of thinking of your life in terms of achieving attainable goals and the very real energizing feeling that comes with it – Let's go **BIG**!

Let's look at some goals with no set time frame. These are things which may seem crazy or improbable, but this is your chance to expand and really dream. Make certain that these reflect YOU - not what your parents, family or employers might want (review your core values). Of course if you have a life partner, you want to consider what he or she wants. Still, make sure that you also remain true to yourself! Here are a few suggestions just to get you started.......

Relationships
ex. read to your child nightly, have 'date nite' with spouse once a month, get married

Things to Learn
ex. Italian cooking, Chess, hang gliding, Python or JavaScript, string theory, driving a 'stick', learn to play guitar

Stacking Paper
ex. get your CPR certification, Master 's degree, Hypnotherapy certification, nursing degree

Creative Stretching
ex. start a blog, write 20 Haiku, draw a landscape or portrait, write a cookbook

Financial Milestones
ex. pay-off a specific credit card, start a college fund for your kids, save $10,000

Sites to Enjoy
ex. Majorca, drive through New England in autumn, Victoria Falls, the Grand Canyon

Business Improvements
ex. start a new company, gain 100 new clients, branch into a new direction

Things to Own
ex. rental income property, a first-edition book, stock shares in a fortune 500, a diamond necklace,

*Q*uite literally anything that you can dream – you can achieve through your matching effort, skill, talent and resources. *But* you have to start by dreaming and then setting smaller goals that will deliver you to the BIG ones!

*M*y Big Picture Goals

*T*he 'STOP' Technique –

Focus, Energize and Heal ~

(based on Johnny 'Ananda' Norman)

*T*his is an extremely simple step that you will begin to use immediately because it gives you such valuable information about where you are (and even more about what's going on around you). This takes about two minutes. The earth will spin without you for a minute or two.

▶ At several points during your day STOP! ~
Wherever you are ~ Whatever you're doing. *STOP!*

▶ Absorb the scene around you ~ what's going on? Take in sights, sounds, colors, odors.

▶ Now take a single deep breath.
In this moment that you are taking for yourself ~ just this moment now ~ there is nothing else for you to think about or accomplish.

▶ Focus, really draw in your awareness ~ check-in with your body:
- ○ Heart rate – really feel your pulse and notice the sensation in your chest
- ○ Breathing – shallow? (from a stuffy nose or is it tension?)
- ○ Skin temperature – are you warm? cool? Is it dry in the room? humid? comfortable?
- ○ Tension - any kinks or knots your body is holding onto

What's the source? ~ is it just a matter of shifting positions or are you stifling the impulse to choke the living daylights out of someone?

▶ Relax your muscles

▶ How do you feel? Happy, bored, hopeful, anxious, rested, frustrated, calm, intimidated, guilty, scattered, accomplished, claustrophobic, at ease ~ Really put a *word* to exactly what you feel in this particular moment.

▸ Now what do you *want* to feel? How would you like to feel ~ *right now?* Would you like to be on a beach somewhere relaxing or out with friends? Is one of the things that you'd like to feel joy?

Leaving behind whatever else you had been doing before or must do after ~ in this moment now ~ conjure for yourself a feeling of warm happiness. You may need to imagine a scene or evoke a memory (although it is better if you can just reach inside and find 'happy' among all the other feelings that you've catalogued in your life).

○ Engage all of your senses – *really sense the Joy rising-up from somewhere inside you.*

○ Smile ~ that's right ~ ear to ear, bring out the gums ~ *Smile!* And *~in this moment~* your feeling will begin changing to feeling good and your body will respond.

What have you noticed while using the 'STOP' Technique?

Deep Breathing

This is such a simple and yet a very powerful, relaxation technique. I'm going to bet that you didn't know that breathing is the only essential bodily function performed unconsciously ~ that you can control consciously? It's true ~ also, your body can go without food for months, water for weeks and yet your body can't go without oxygen for more than a few minutes. Think about it.

Your breath is quite literally your life force. Oxygen feeds every part of your body. So merely the act of breathing influences every single organ in your body and balances your brain hemispheres. Approximately 90% of all of your energy is created by oxygen and nearly all of your body's actions are regulated by it. This makes it rather important to get enough of it!!

Yet, most of us don't get enough. We tend to do what's called shallow breathing. In fact, shallow breathing can often be a symptom of stress. Similarly, shallow breathing can result in fatigue and stress due to the intake of insufficient oxygen.

It is surprising how few of us actually breathe 'properly'. Breathing is something we take for granted. However, shallow breathing can often be a symptom of stress. Similarly, it can result in fatigue and stress due to the intake of insufficient oxygen.

There is a lot more information on this in my book 'The Biology of Beating Stress'. Anytime you're tired, stop and take ten deep breaths. While we're at it ~ let's optimize the way you take them. The best way to breathe is in the pit (or bottom) of your stomach. *Why?* Few people realize that their lungs extend beyond their rib cage, in fact ⅔ of your lungs sit below the lowest rib. Filling this larger portion of your lungs will literally enhance your energy.

Deep breathing has been used for literally centuries and is the cornerstone of many other relaxation practices from different cultures around the world. You'll find they can very readily be combined with other relaxing elements such as aromatherapy and music.

Here you'll find several techniques which are easy to learn, can be practiced almost anywhere, and provide a quick way to get your stress levels back in check.

The Basic 'Belly Breath'
(or Diaphragmatic Breathing):

You may have become more accustomed to only feeling your chest rise and fall as you breathe, that's shallow breathing, but this is a little different. So, just to get a basic understanding of it until you can do it instinctively ~ place your hand on your stomach just below your navel.

Sit in a comfortable position with your hands on your knees. Relax your shoulders. Breathing through your nose ~ inhale ~ let your relaxed stomach muscles drop while filling this lower area of your stomach with air ~ as deeply as you can (try counting slowly to five). At the bottom of your breath, pause for two counts. Then breathe out through your mouth (again try counting to five). Now close your eyes and repeat 5–10 times.

A really immediate way to experience diaphragmatic or belly breathing is to simply lie on your back and breathe ~ your body will do it automatically from this position.

Why? Did you know that your lungs don't actually have muscle of their own? Your lungs are just like two loose empty sacks - they cannot draw air in on their own. The movement of your diaphragm, (a large muscle that separates the rib cage and its organs from the abdominal cavity) draws air in and out of your body. Your diaphragm works like a bellows.

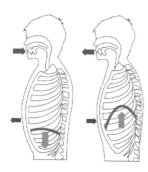

As your diaphragm moves down from the base of the ribs, air is drawn through the nostrils, through the trachea and bronchial tubes, and into the many small sacs linking the lungs. As air is drawn into the lungs, they fill and expand, expanding the rib cage, lifting the surface of the abdomen up. A more controlled and conscious movement of the diaphragm draws air more deeply into the lungs.

*P*ursed Lip Breathing (PLB)

*T*his terrific exercise elongates the breath through resistance.

Why would you want to do this to reduce stress?? Because it is an easy way to not only slow your respiration in a way that opens the airwaves and improves your lung function but, this simple exercise also quickly reduces anxiety and increases mental performance. PLB has also been shown to alleviate dyspnea, the shortness of breath resulting from abnormal heart or lung function. Reportedly it:

- Improves ventilation
- Keeps your airways open longer and decreases the work of breathing
- Prolongs exhalation to slow your breathing rate
- Relieves shortness of breath
- Causes general relaxation

Caution: Do not hold do this if you have high blood pressure.

The Step by Step:

Sit comfortably. Your back should be well supported but, relaxed. Release any tension in your neck and shoulder muscles. Your feet should touch the floor or be supported comfortably.

1. Breathe in (inhale) slowly through your nose for two counts, keeping your mouth closed.
(Don't take a deep breath; a normal breath will do).
   While you inhale:
   - Place both hands on your lower stomach (or abdomen).
   - Spread your fingers out.
   - Concentrate on expanding lower abdomen (diaphragm) as you inhale through your nose.

2. Exhale with tight lips ~ gently press the center of your lips together and permit the air to escape through both sides of the lips ~ as if you're trying to inflate a very tight balloon. Make exhaling slower and longer than inhaling (Should be two or three times (and occasionally four times) longer than inspiration.

40

As you exhale:

- Please remember to contract your stomach muscles as you are pushing the air out.

- Do not force the air out, but DO feel a sense of pressure as if blowing through a pin sized straw.

Continue breathing in this way until you notice a sense of calm moving into your body.

Why is this Method So Effective?

Resistance created by breathing out through tightened lips:

○ Naturally slows down your breathing rate. By allowing your airways to remain open for just a few more seconds, you are able to exhale more fully, and do a better job of getting rid of carbon dioxide. This, in turn, affects how much oxygen will actually make it into your bloodstream.

○ Creates a 'back pressure' that helps open your airways.

○ Strengthens and improves overall lung function and also increases your lung capacity.

NOTE: Practice inhaling and exhaling a few times to simply become familiar with the feeling of the slower exhalations. If at any time you begin to feel faint, dizzy, flushed or light-headed, **stop** and allow your breath to return to its natural rhythm. These other sensations are generally the result of the increased oxygen levels in your body, which you may not be accustomed to.

This technique allows you to literally "fill" your lungs with oxygen and because the richest blood flow in your lungs is at the bottom (where they are the largest) you will now be flooding your body with both oxygen and energy.

Breathing deeply and evenly through both nostrils has been reported to help synchronize both sides of the brain. The right nostril tends to stimulate the left side of the brain and the left stimulates the right side of the brain.[2]

Research has proven that the brain swaps the dominate nostril you breathe through every 90 minutes. In fact, some physicians consider the breath as the doorway between your conscious and your unconscious mind. Breathing exercises like Alternate Nostril Breathing[3] can potentially help both to relax and feed specific parts of the body, while possibly giving greater control over your nervous system.

Alternate Nostril Breathing
(Pranayama - Naadi Shodhana)

This is going to knock your *socks off!*

Again, so simple ~ so easy to do. Just 3 – 5 minutes twice a day.

A study done by Andrej Stančák Jr. suggested that this easy technique actually has a balancing effect on the functional activity of the left and right hemisphere.[3]

Caution: Do not hold your breath if you have high blood pressure. Confirm with your doctor before beginning any new exercise or activity like this one.

The Step by Step:

Sit in a comfortable position. Relax.

- ☞ Place your right thumb on the right side of your nose, in that little groove where your nostril flares
- ☞ GENTLY press your right nostril closed with your right thumb
- ☞ *Gently* exhale slowly through the left nostril
- ☞ Then inhale softly & slowly through your left nostril

- ☞ Close your left nostril with your right ring finger, release your thumb, and exhale gently & slowly through your right nostril
- ☞ Inhale slowly through your right nostril
- ☞ Now, close your right nostril with your thumb, exhale left nostril

Continue with this rhythmic breathing, slowly and smoothly, inhaling fully, exhaling completely. *Relax.*

Stretching

*T*hese gentle movements emphasize concentration, relaxation and also conscious circulation of vital energy throughout your body. Fear, anger and frustration all register in your body's muscles. Experience tells us unreleased stress can result in back aches, headaches, tense muscles, muscle spasms and a not-so-jolly disposition.

We hold tension in various parts of our bodies due to stress, without any awareness of discomfort ~ the discomfort can even become our 'norm'. We've just adapted to being tense. Here's a little quote from Steven Wolf, Associate Professor in the Department of Physical and Rehabilitative Medicine at Emory University School of Medicine in Atlanta, "People in tense, sedentary jobs are particularly prone to a chronic shortening of the muscles". He went on to say, "Without even realizing it, they hold their bodies in a tense, alert pose day after day. 'The buildup continues each day as the tensions repeat. As time goes on, their neck and shoulder muscles get shorter and shorter." Wolf is both a physical therapist and a neurophysiologist.[2]

Even mild muscle tension can build overtime into a knot of excruciating pain. When your muscle tightens, the tension slows blood flow in that area. Usually, blood flow washes away all the byproducts of metabolic activity, but if your muscle stays consistently tense, it becomes oxygen-starved and metabolites, like lactic acid will build-up. You've got pain receptors in your muscles which are sensitive both to shortening of the muscle fibers and to any build-up of metabolites. *Guess what?* When these pain receptors detect such conditions, they send a message of pain to your brain.

Stretching releases tension being held in your muscles. Practiced regularly, it can also strengthen the Relaxation Response[10], in your daily life.

Stretching actually stimulates receptors in your nervous system that decrease production of stress hormones. *That's right.* It turns that little switch in your brain that says, "We're in danger!" to the off position. Think about it. By relieving pent-up tension in your large muscle groups it signals your brain that there is no emergency.

Combine your stretching with a little deep breathing and the alert is pretty much deemed unnecessary ~ it gives the 'all-clear' signal to your brain. Your body can go back to all of its normal functions.

Overall, the increase that stretching creates in your flexibility will improve your performance in everyday physical tasks, such as bending down to pick up a pen, running to catch a bus, lifting heavy objects, etc. The gains that stretching gives you in range of motion will improve your general balance, making you less prone to accidental slips and falls that become more likely with increasing age.

Since injuries can happen when stretching is done incorrectly, it's best that you learn in a group class, work with a private instructor or at the very least following video instructions.

Always tune into your body and be gentle when stretching. Do not stretch your muscles to the point of actual pain ~ stretch only to the point of minimal discomfort.

Never start your workout with stretching! The American Council on Exercise points out that you should never stretch cold muscles. A slight warm-up session (meaning just enough to make you start a slight sweat and to breathe heavier) is what you need before stretching.

Qi Slap Warm-up: Reportedly for centuries this technique has been used to bring blood flow to the skin, help loosen stagnations and toxins from the muscles and cells and generally wake up your internal systems. Lightly slap the areas below in a soft and gentle yet, vigorous, fashion. Give just a few seconds to each area.

You can finish all 9 areas in just a minute or two.

1. briskly slap just at the top of the ribcage to wake-up your thyroid gland in a simultaneous rhythm.

2. continue the motion on your chest with an alternating rhythm.

3. briskly slap moving one hand under one arm down the side of your ribs; then do the other side.

4. use one hand, slap down the inside of one arm to your palm, then up the outside of your hand and arm to your shoulder. Use an alternating rhythm. Second arm likewise.

5. use an alternating rhythm to gently slap your cheeks, forehead and sides of the head to the top of your skull, down the back of the cranium, and down your neck.

6. continue the motion on your stomach with an alternating rhythm.

7. briskly slap your lower back and kidneys with both hands (alternating side to side each slap) and down to the sacrum.

8. use both hands slapping down the outside of your legs in a simultaneous rhythm.

9. gently slap down the back of your legs in a simultaneous rhythm. Then do the front and inside

CAUTION: - When NOT to Stretch:

- After a recent fracture
- When either joints or muscles are hurt, infected or in any way inflamed
- Following muscle strains or ligament sprains
- Whenever sharp pains are felt in your joints or muscles

Now, let's talk about a few ways to loosen-up!

Simple Hamstring Stretch

Static stretching which means stretching a body part to its farthest position and then holding it for just about 30 seconds. It doesn't involve any bouncing or rapid movements, just a mild, painless pulling sensation. You should feel the stretch through the entire length and center of the muscle but, not in the joints.

Always, always confirm with your doctor before beginning any new exercise or activity like this one.

The Step by Step

- In lose clothing ~ Sit on the ground and put both legs in front of you in a 'V' shape.

- Take both hands and gently reach for your right foot. You should feel a gentle stretch through the backside of your leg (especially the hamstring). Feel the release through your lower back and shoulders. Bring your head down to touch your knee.

   Don't bounce ~ this should be a relaxed, smooth motion.

   Hold only for a slow count of three and come up.

- Reach for your left foot and repeat this very gentle stretch.

Gradually, as you repeat the motion lightly and smoothly 10 – 20 times, alternating from one side to the other you'll notice that you're able to bring your head lower more comfortably.

*U*ttanasana (OOT-tan-AHS-ahna) – 'Brain Bath'

*I*n Sanskrit, "ut" means intense, "tan" means to stretch or extend and "asana" means pose.

Let's see….would you be interested in something reported to:

- **Reduce stress, anxiety, depression and fatigue**

- **Calm your mind and soothe the nerves**

- **Relieve tension in the spine, neck and back**

- **Activate your abdominal muscles**

- **Ease symptoms of menopause, asthma, headache and insomnia**

- **Stimulate your kidneys, liver, spleen**

- **Improve digestion**

- **May lower high blood pressure**

- **Therapeutic for infertility, osteoporosis and sinusitis**

- **Stretch your hips, hamstrings and calves**

- **Strengthen your thighs and knees**

- **Keep your spine strong and flexible**

Why did I nickname this the 'Brain Bath'?

Inverting in this easy way gives your heart a break. Your heart works every second to ensure that freshly oxygenated blood makes its way up to your precious brain and its sensory organs. This pose very naturally rejuvenates your mental alertness and energy while improving your overall blood circulation. So when inverting, the pressure differential across your entire body is partially reversed and blood floods to the brain with little work from your heart.

But another great benefit of Uttanasana is that it very gently stretches your large leg muscles, (where most of us generally hold a great deal of our tension). And *guess what?* For this reason Uttanasaana has a deeply relaxing effect. It can calm your entire nervous system and relieves stress, anxiety and insomnia.[13]

Other physical benefits reportedly can include decompressing the spine, improving your circulation and boosting your digestion, metabolic and your endocrine system which along with the hormones it releases influences almost every cell, organ, and function of your body.[12] The endocrine system is instrumental in regulating mood, growth and development, tissue function and metabolism, as well as sexual function and reproductive processes.

Actually there are four major systems in your body that the practice of inversions positively influences: cardiovascular, lymphatic, nervous and endocrine.

Biology 101: Your circulatory system is amazing. It of course includes your heart, lungs and the complete system of vessels that both send oxygen as well as, collect carbon dioxide and other waste products that your cells release. You've got an entire network of arteries fanning out in an intricate pipe system away from your heart, which pumps much needed freshly oxygenated blood from your lungs outward. Your veins return the blood to your heart and (unlike your arteries), create a low-pressure system that depends on either muscular movement or gravity to move your blood along. at regular intervals all along this system, one-way valves prevent backwash and keep precious fluids moving always towards your heart in a system known as 'venous return.'

Some believe that turning yourself upside down (inversion positions like headstands, handstands and uttanasana) will encourage this venous return which is why it can be effective at supporting your overall blood circulation.

Inversions may also help to ensure improved and more effective lung tissue. Gravity comes into play here again. As you stand or sit upright (especially for long periods), gravity will naturally pull all of your fluids downward, which is thought to cause blood to saturate your lower lungs more thoroughly. This would in turn cause your lower lung tissue to be more compressed than that of your upper lungs. So while the air you inhale moves naturally into the open alveoli of your upper lungs; unless you're regularly taking good, deep breaths, you can't really raise the balance of air to the

52

blood in your lower lungs. *Not Good.* But, when you invert, even just moderately, blood will perfuse your now well-ventilated lung upper lobes, and then ensure that you get more efficient oxygen-to-blood exchange and healthier lung tissue. Yay!

The Step by Step:

🖝 Gently raise your arms overhead, turning the palms to face each other.

🖝 Exhale and bend forward slowly from your hip joints, (not from your waist) until your hands are in line with your feet. Maintain the length through your spine, maintaining this forward bend from the pelvis only, not from your lower back.

🖝 If possible, with your knees soft or straight, gently bring your palms or finger tips to the floor slightly in front of or beside your feet or bring your palms to the backs of your ankles. Make certain to keep your heels pressed down.

Note: If this isn't possible, *don't worry.* Just cross your forearms and hold your elbows (bend your knees if you have to). Really just hang there ~ gravity will do the rest.

○ Stay in this pose approximately 30 seconds to 1 minute.

With each inhalation during the pose, lift and lengthen your front torso just slightly; with each exhalation release a little more fully into your forward bend. This helps your torso to oscillate (very faintly) with each breath. Let your head hang from the root of your neck, which is deep in the upper back, between your shoulder blades.

Don't roll your spine to come up. Instead just bring your hands back onto your hips and gently, gradually, one vertebra at a time, lift and lengthen your front torso while pressing your tailbone down and into the pelvis and come-up during an inhalation.

If you do decide to try this or any inversion therapy, as a rule, start slowly for no more than 5 minutes at a time.

Very Important Cautions:
People with heart disease, high blood pressure, circulatory conditions, eye diseases (such as glaucoma), digestive issues such as heartburn, or are pregnant are at higher risk for the dangers related to this or any kind of inversion therapy. Being upside down places a great deal of stress on the circulatory system.

This pose is not recommended for people with low back problems without the guidance of an experienced yoga teacher.

Also, for people with tight hamstrings Uttanasana can be contraindicated, because if not done properly, the pose puts stress on the lower back.

The first time anyone tries any kind inversion therapy, you should be sure to have someone standing by, in case assistance is required or if health problems are experienced.

Everyone should always confirm with their doctor before beginning any new exercise or activity like this one.

*M*ovement

A lot has been learned through the benefit of technology. Major improvements have been made in what we now know about how are bodies respond under stress and, also how are bodies respond to exercise ~ and for years we've been operating under some wrong assumptions. We've been exercising *TOO LONG!!*

Your body was designed for movement. You can't avoid it. Every functional system in your body requires energy propelled by movement. Remember too, that if you're under routine stress (of any kind – mental, physical, emotional), – you need the release that comes through exercise. *Yes!* You have to exercise! But, how much?!

Here's the good news!! After you've been cleared by your doctor, consider High-Intensity Interval Training (HIT) as your primary exercise.[5] You'll do this for twenty minutes just three times a week. Yep! 20 minutes – 3x a week.

*H*ow Does High Intensity Interval Training Affect Our Bodies?

1. You improve your fitness level, your ability to utilize oxygen. The more oxygen you're able to use, the more calories you burn.

2. Interval-training workouts widen the network of blood vessels that supply muscles and boost the number of mitochondria (structures that produce energy within the body's cells), thereby increasing endurance, according to the McMaster researchers.

3. Because of changes that actually happen inside your cells, you increase post-exercise fat burning and calorie expenditure, even during rest or sleep. Yes, that means you literally burn more calories *while you sleep!*

4. You can naturally increase your Human Growth Hormone (HGH) levels, which promotes fat burning and muscle building.

The "secret" to why HIT is so effective is clear. According to fitness expert Phil Campbell author of the book *'Ready Set Go'*:

"Most exercise programs today are built based upon a very incomplete picture of the physiology of your body. For example, long slow cardio, "calories in, calories out," would be a perfect way to look at the body if it were all slow-twitch fiber … [but] there are three muscle fiber types: slow, fast and super-fast … both those types of fast-twitch fibers are essentially 50 percent of your muscle fibers that don't get recruited until you add a velocity of movement."

So, if you don't actively engage and strengthen all three muscle fiber types (and energy systems), then you're simply not going to work both processes of your heart muscle. Unfortunately, many believe that cardio exercise employs your heart muscle – that's really not true. What you're actually working is your slow twitch muscle fibers. You're not effectively engaging the anaerobic process of your heart.

Those fast-twitch fibers are largely glycolytic and they store a lot of glucose. That's right, good ole' *sugar.* So when these muscles are employed, it not only creates the stimulus needed to actually grow more muscle, it also enlarges the glucose storage reservoir in your muscle, which in turn boost your insulin sensitivity. This is the secret behind why one of the primary health benefits of HIT exercise is normalizing your insulin. Conventional aerobics simply won't do this as efficiently.

Have a look at the evidence. There have been many studies done which more than support the 'less is more' paradigm shift. Although other studies have shown that High Intensity Interval Training can markedly improve your overall fitness and athletic performance, still little was known about how it affects your energy expenditure, which is kind of an factor that motivates many people to exercise in the first place ~ the desire to burn calories.

So, to determine just how many calories a typical High Intensity Interval workout (which they call 'sprint interval training' might burn, Kyle Sevits of Colorado State University and his colleagues recruited five healthy male volunteers, all between the ages of 25 and 31 years old. Initially, these volunteers performed an exercise stress test to make sure their hearts were healthy enough to participate. The researchers also analyzed the volunteers' body compositions and their resting metabolic rates.

Then, over the next three days, the volunteers ate a diet precisely adjusted to meet their metabolic needs so that they'd be in "energy balance," Sevits explains, with just enough calories so that they weren't over or under-eating.

On day four, the men then checked-in to a research facility at the University of Colorado Anschultz Medical Campus. Although each room was outfitted much like any standard hospital room, it was completely enclosed; with air intake and exhaust regulated and also specialized equipment was installed to analyze oxygen, carbon dioxide and water content. Based on the results of this analysis, the researchers could easily check to see just how many calories the volunteers actually burned while in their isolation.

For two full days, each volunteer lived in confinement continuing to eat the prescribed diet and spending most of their time pretty much at rest, watching movies or using a computer. However, on one of the days, they were asked to engage in a 'sprint interval workout' that involved pedaling as fast as possible on a stationary bicycle in the room that was set at a high resistance for five 30-second periods, each separated by four-minute periods of recovery in which they pedaled slowly with only a small amount of resistance.

Their results were clear. There was a major increase in the amount of calories burned on workout day, despite the short amount of time that they spent in actual hard exercise. The research revealed that exercisers can burn as many as 200 extra calories in as little as 2.5 minutes of concentrated effort per day ~ as long as they mix it up with longer periods of easy recovery. The finding could make exercise more manageable for those *would-be* fitness buffs by cramming truly intense efforts into as little as 25 minutes.

SOooooooo How's it Done?

VERY IMPORTANT CAUTION: Before beginning any new exercise consult your doctor. Some conditions & health considerations are potentially serious and should be evaluated by a qualified healthcare provider.

*H*igh Intensity Interval Training

Ultimately here you want to exercise energetically enough so that you reach your anaerobic threshold because this is where the "magic" happens that will trigger your growth hormone release.

1. 3 minute warm-up
2. 30 seconds at Full Intensity (respiration increases, feel muscles burning, profuse sweating occurs by the 2nd or 3rd repetition)
3. 90 seconds Medium Pace (respiration should recover)
4. Repeat steps 2 and 3 just seven times
5. Finish with 5 minute Cool-Down

It can also be done on a recumbent bike, elliptical trainer, in-line skates, mini-trampoline or even with squat thrusts.

If you're not in great shape and just starting this you may want to start with just two or three repetitions and work your way up to eight. Don't be brave or daring.

Note: there is absolutely no real benefit to going beyond eight repetitions. I know you're thinking the more you do the quicker you'll get into shape but, not so....

Recovery Time in Between Sessions is Crucial

Yep! You really have to take a day-off between HIT sessions. This recovery time is crucial to allowing your body to replenish energy stores and repair damaged soft tissues (muscles, tendons, ligaments) and the removal of chemicals that build-up as a result of cell activity during exercise.

Remember that exercise (or really any other physical work) will cause changes in your body such as muscle tissue breakdown and the depletion of energy stores (muscle glycogen) as well as fluid loss. Giving your body a day in-between allows these stores to be replenished and allows tissue repair to occur. Symptoms of overtraining often occur from a lack of rest days and recovery time.

*H*ow are Conventional Cardio or Aerobic Exercises and the Anaerobic Exercise of HIT Different?

Without getting too technical - while oxygen is used to break down glucose by aerobic exercise, the anaerobic exercises make use of phosphocreatine, stored in the muscles, for the same process.

Aerobic exercises concentrate on strengthening and the muscles involved in respiration. It improves the circulation of blood and transportation of oxygen in the body, reduces blood pressure and burns fat.

On the other hand, anaerobic exercise helps build strength and muscle mass, stronger bones and increases speed, power, muscle strength and the metabolic rate as well. It concentrates on burning the calories, when the body is in rest. *How?* Doing HIT will increase your resting metabolic rate (RMR) in the 24 hours following the workout. That's right! Even after you're done with exercise, more calories are burned off. *You gotta luv that.*

But, be prepared: You're need to work really hard during your high-intensity periods to make this a fat-burning workout – probably much harder than you're accustomed to – hence getting checked out by your doctor <u>first</u>. To avoid injury, increase intensity only in small increments every 7-10 days, but no more. If you're not an experienced exerciser or if you have any physical issues, don't go all-out – aim for moderate exertion, enough to raise your breathing rate. You'll still get benefits without risking injury.

*W*eighty Matters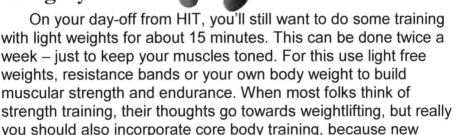

On your day-off from HIT, you'll still want to do some training with light weights for about 15 minutes. This can be done twice a week – just to keep your muscles toned. For this use light free weights, resistance bands or your own body weight to build muscular strength and endurance. When most folks think of strength training, their thoughts go towards weightlifting, but really you should also incorporate core body training, because new muscle tissue is produced whenever your muscle cells are required to lift something heavy on a repetitive basis. You can start small, doing just a few push-ups or stretches before going to bed and

60

learning exercises you can do using resistance bands. A University of Michigan study proved that after an average of eighteen to twenty weeks of progressive resistance training, an adult can add 2.42 pounds of lean muscle to their body mass and increase overall strength 25 to 30 percent.[6]

Ok, a little bad news - On average you'll lose 5 percent of your muscle mass every 10 years after the age of 35—if you don't do some sort of training. Over 10 years, a person easily can lose two and a half pounds of muscle! Not Good!

Remember muscle is used to burn fat – so this muscle loss results also in increased difficulty for you to maintain your ideal weight. You no longer have sufficient muscle mass to burn the calories you consume. So, if you don't deliberately rebuild your muscle through exercise, you'll need to eat 150 to 450 fewer calories every day every 10 years to maintain your current weight. *Ouch!*

"Healthy muscle is not only about being stronger and bigger," says Miriam Nelson, director of the John Hancock Center for Physical Activity and Nutrition at Tufts University. Strength training that builds muscle helps keep older folks stable and surefooted and strong enough to do basic things like get out of a chair. "A 70-year-old active individual is probably younger from a biomarker standpoint - muscle strength, balance, body composition, blood pressure, cholesterol levels - than a 40-year-old inactive individual," said Dr. Nelson. Her landmark research demonstrated that previously sedentary postmenopausal women who lifted weights twice a week for a year could increase their muscle strength by about 80 percent.[14] *Are you motivated yet?* We're talking about a 15 minute commitment twice a week!

Maintaining muscle also requires getting an adequate amount of protein from your diet as mentioned earlier in Chapter 4. A 2009 study conducted by Paddon-Jones found that four ounces of lean beef, eaten immediately after a resistance training workout, boosted the body's muscle-building rate by 50 percent in both young and older people.[15] By the way, he also found that eating 12 ounces of beef didn't provide any extra benefits. Remember, other excellent sources of protein include wild salmon, halibut, cod, lentils, black beans, walnuts, almonds and quinoa.

But also in your exercise routine - mix-it-up every now and then ~ your brain is designed to always conserve as much energy as possible and diversity, will keep it varying how much to use. Go for a walk or dance to boost your energy, mood and cardiovascular health. Do Yoga, Tai chi or stretching to relax and improve yo'r flexibility. Actually, try to sweat profusely at least three times ι week to release toxins – steam in your shower or use a sauna.

But, as always, check with your doctor before beginning an, new health regimen.

*E*xercise & What 2 Eat – When?

Remember, when you don't have proper nutrition – when you don't feed yourself, it puts your body under stress to function optimally – which will contribute subliminally to any other stress you may have. So, when it comes to exercise and the questions become, 'To eat or not to eat?' 'Before or after?' *Both!* I'll explain.

Before Exercise:

The research is in – and it shows that exercising after short-term fasting (such as before breakfast) may increase the amount of fat you burn. On the other hand, eating a meal which stimulates a low blood glucose response prior to exercise may also boost the actual use of body fat (instead of glucose). Research further shows that if you exercise for longer than 60 minutes without supplying your body with any nutrients, you will actually burn fewer calories and even less fat than if you had eaten, and your post exercise metabolic rate, or rate of calorie burning, is also lower.

hmmmmm let's just use common sense – shall we?

You've got several factors to consider, specifically, how long you exercise, your type of exercise, your exercise experience level and health factors that may play a role in how you process food. That said, you know that IF you eat, you would need to allow time for the food to digest before exercising (otherwise you'll cramp, right?). Also, you know that more time is needed before more intense activities.

Large meal: > 3-4 hrs.
Small meal: 2-3 hrs.
Liquid meal: 1-2 hrs.
Light snack: < 1 hr

Again, wearing our 'common sense' hat – when you stop to consider the amount of time that it takes to digest even a light snack, you can without difficulty conclude that the majority of the "fuel" that you'll use during most exercise is really not coming from the food you've just eaten. Nope. You're using glycogen and fat that was already stored in your muscles, liver and fat cells.

Usually, you'll have enough of that stored fuel to last for one to two hours of intense to very intense exercise or three to four of moderate intensity. So technically – you're covered without eating. *But*, when you don't eat at all, you then risk breaking down muscle and causing a great deal of stress to your body during exercise. Conclusion….

So, keeping all of what we've just reviewed in mind – doesn't it just make sense to have a regular meal 4 hours prior to a workout, followed by a small 200 calorie snack one hour before exercise?

Keep it light. Pre-workout you don't want to have large amounts proteins and fats (even if they're healthy proteins and fats). These types of fuels take a long time to digest and draw precious oxygen and energy-delivering blood to your stomach and away from your exercising muscles. They also carry a greater risk of giving you stomach cramps during your exercise.

Choose whole foods, not sports drinks, energy bars or powders which will only add hazardous toxins, chemicals and useless calories, sugar and caffeine to your diet.

✓ Hydrate with filtered water having at least 16 oz. 2 hrs. earlier and another 8 oz. 10-20 min. right before exercise.

200 calories may be hard to visualize, so consider:

Raw nuts (walnuts, almonds, pistachios) (½ cup)

Brown rice (½ cup) with black beans (½ cup)

Banana with almond butter (2 Tbsp)

Multi-grain crackers (10) with hummus (3 Tbsp)

After Exercise:

Food eaten after your workout can be a big influence on the overall health effects that exercise creates. You don't want to have done all of that work for nothing! Your goal is not to replace every calorie that you've just burned, but to give you just enough fuel so that you can maintain a high yielding metabolism.

After a workout with weights - wait just 15-30 minutes and then have a high-quality protein (whole food) and vegetable-type carbohydrate; in order to help repair your damaged muscles.

After cardio - wait 45-60 minutes, and likewise have a high-quality protein (whole food) and vegetable-type carbohydrate.

✓ Hydrate well after both with an electrolyte balanced water – have at least 16 oz. (preferably 24 oz.)

Protein provides essential amino acids which are the building blocks for muscle repair and growth. From current research it seems that eating specifically fewer carbohydrates after exercise can actually enhance your insulin sensitivity, compared to simply reducing calorie intake. Optimizing your insulin sensitivity is so important for maintaining good health.

After you've exercised your muscles have been broken down due to the release of hormones, and your body is nitrogen-poor. This is when it becomes important to provide your body with the correct nutrients to stop the catabolic process happening in your muscles and shift the whole recycling process over towards muscle repair and growth. When you miss that window of opportunity to feed your muscles at the right time after exercise, that entire catabolic process will go too far and can potentially damage your muscles. Amino acids from high quality animal proteins, along with carbohydrates from vegetables (not grains) are absolutely necessary for this process.

Good sources of animal protein include:
- Kefir (Organic, Plain)
- Eggs (Organic, from pastured hens)
- Chicken (Organic, Humanely raised, Free-range)
- Beef (Organic, Grass-fed)
- Hemp, Rice or Pea Protein (for our vegetarian friends)

Remember that portion size should be very limited to between 2 – 4oz.

Favorable sources of carbohydrates include:

- All vegetables (especially dark green, leafy vegetables such as organic spinach, kale or Swiss chard *BUT* limiting carrots and beets, which are high in sugar)

- Low fructose fruits like organic lemon, limes, grapefruit, passion fruit, apricots, plums, cantaloupe & raspberries.

  *Avoid high fructose fruits like cherries, grapes, apples, watermelons and pears

*F*ood

A really helpful tool is keeping a Food Diary. This is not a 'Monitor for Guilt' or a 'Journal of Shame' ~ *far from it.* Your food diary is your friend because it will (and there's lots of evidence to back this up) help you be more aware of your actual eating, activity habits, problem areas and most importantly ~ how you feel after eating.

That's right we're so busy stuffing our faces and then getting back to whatever the whole 'eating thing' has interrupted that we can't be bothered to take note of responses our body is having to the food we 'inhale'. We don't know how effective the foods we chose are at really satisfying our hunger. We don't even really monitor our digestion difficulties ~ unless they become problematic. Then suddenly we take an interest and start to blame our foods when sometimes it's the combination of ~ well yes, the 'crappy' foods with 'crappy' moods that we're in when we consume them!

Noticing the way that you feel physically and emotionally before, during and after each meal, snack or beverage gives you important information. This is another area where more 'Being' and less stress come into play. Your emotional state as you're eating directly affects the way that your body cells utilize the nutrients, chemicals and energy in your food.

Start each of your meals with three deep breaths. Simply stop yourself for that moment and breathe…. Simplistic yes and it will have a major impact. You're probably thinking – 'I barely have time to eat – much less stop and breathe.' Well, that's the point. Slow things down – your body will thank you. This goes for families too. Yes, it's already hard enough to get them to all sit down together for a meal, but you're teaching them habits for a lifetime. *A lifetime.*

So wrangle them in as often as possible to sit down for a meal and tell them we are going to have a moment of silence and take three deep breaths before we eat. It's something new – so of course you may get protests, wiggling, giggling – but, eventually it will become just a part of their routine – simple habits – like reaching for your hand as they approach a street corner or brushing teeth before bed.

Your friend the food diary will of course also encourage you to make conscious choices about what you eat, where you eat (for instance not at your work desk) and to look back and see what you've changed over time. Writing this down gives you the chance to think twice before you eat. This is one of the most useful things you can do to help you gain control your weight, improve your digestion and reduce your stress.

*E*motional Eating

Consider also when you might be eating for emotional reasons – did someone tick-you-off and you reached for chocolate? Did your mother phone and suddenly you've gotten a craving for pastry or a down-home (very calorically heavy) meal? SOoooo many people self-medicate with food. It's used to fend-off loneliness, depression, anger, frustration and *STRESS.*

We have all succumbed to sometimes using food for comfort, distraction or just because we're bored. Every now and then turning to food to celebrate an occasion or forget your troubles doesn't mean that you have a problem. *However*, habitually letting your emotions dictate what and when you eat can not only pack on the pounds, but also create other health issues if left unresolved.

Experts state that much of emotional eating stems from childhood, where a majority of us learned to associate food with comfort. You can easily picture it: a crying baby offered a bottle or a breast; a 5-year-old who skins their knee given a cookie as a treat. But also, eating is a common distraction which lets you escape ~ even if temporarily ~ from your problems.

Just based on your own experience you can probably report how ~ emotions such as anger, unhappiness or loneliness may cause you to eat, consciously or unconsciously, in an effort to block those feelings. Everyone feels badly at one point or another, but not everyone turns to food to self-soothe. This is where your friend the Food Diary is going to help you uncover any unfortunate eating patterns which you may have picked-up over the years.

Your first step is figuring out which emotions trigger you to eat. You can't possibly know this if every day you just mindlessly eat without any acknowledgement of how you were feeling (physically and emotionally) surrounding your meal.

Keeping a quick little food journal will help you do this very easily because you will write down ~ when you ate, what you ate, how you felt, whether you were physically hungry and how you felt afterward. Only with this information can you begin to help deal with any issues and create alternative behaviors to work them out ~ instead of eating.

Please keep in mind that it will take a little practice for you to develop this new "muscle" allowing you to be able to withstand negative feelings without mindlessly grabbing that chocolate bar, bag of salty chips or creamy ice cream treat. You've had *years* of practice covering-up your emotions with food, so expect an occasional setback, but know that over time, as you develop new habits you will improve your emotional and physical health.

Stop and think ~ then make better choices. Learn to fuel your body for optimal energy, fitness and health!

*And.....*What's on that Plate??

Try, as often as possible to balance the food on your plate. Let's compare carbohydrates to putting gasoline in your car – fast energy. Proteins are your breaks - they slow down the 'carbs' you consume – so you're not hungry as quickly! A good protein portion size is about the size of your fist. And actually it's about the same for your carbohydrate. You will want to have a protein; 'carb' *and yes*, something raw or deep green on your plate at every meal.

We talked a little bit about this on page 8 with regards to Your fasting insulin level, but again any meal or snack that you eat which is high in carbohydrates will also generate a quick rise in your blood glucose. Now - to adjust for this rapid rise, your pancreas will secrete insulin into your bloodstream, which swiftly lowers your levels of blood glucose. Why is that a bad thing? - Because, insulin is essentially a "storage" hormone. Early on, your body evolved this insulin as a way to store excess carbohydrate calories in the form of fat, *just in case* there were times of famine. So, the insulin that's stimulated by excess carbohydrates aggressively stimulates your accumulation of body fat! Not Good.

So each time you eat too much sugar (including bread, pasta starchy vegetables or any other grain product) - your body gets the hormonal message (via insulin), "Hey, store some more fat." This is

68

a great benefit for certain parts of the world or during periods when calories are very scarce – but, is part of the cause of our obesity epidemic here in the US.

Basically, you will want to:
- O   Avoid all hydrogenated oils and sugars
- O   Increase raw vegetable intake
- O   Consume at least 25g of fiber per day
- O   Limit Alcohol Consumption
- O   Consider Dietary Supplementation

Veggies vs. ....*Everything Else You'd Rather Eat*

Fact: Eating at least one third of your diet as raw food is good. An even better choice is to eat a diet based on 80 percent fresh organic vegetables, seeds, raw nuts and a little organic fruit, helps to put your body into an alkaline environment (meaning it's very balanced and *very, very happy*). Your organic vegetables provide live enzymes and phytonutrients that are easily absorbed and reach down to the cellular level to nourish and enhance growth of healthy cells.

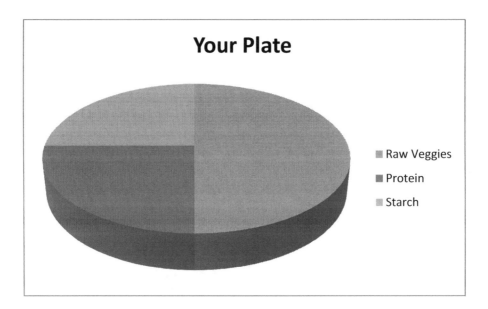

About 20 percent of your diet can be from cooked food (including beans and legumes, whole grain breads, pastas, black or brown rice). Raw, is so important as a factor in your vegetable choice. Why? because it provides you with essential dietary fiber to assist in proper digestion and good bowel habits. You probably chuckled at this when I mentioned this earlier but, it will make a huge difference in your health.

Enzymes and phytonutrients are destroyed at temperatures of 104 degrees F (40 degrees C) - so cooked vegetables which can provide good dietary fiber, still don't contain as much of the valuable nutrients and none of the enzymes that your body needs. The same, by the way, applies to frozen vegetables. Now just imagine how this information applies to those yummy frozen meals that you nuke in your microwave! *Yep!* The cardboard box it came in is almost equal in nutritional value.

Studies reveal that when you eat a majority of cooked foods you are consuming acidic toxins faster than your body can eliminate them which disrupt your body's delicate acid/alkaline balance, becoming a major contributor to excess weight and disease. Heating food above 118 degrees F (47.78 degrees C) causes chemical changes that create acidic toxins, including the carcinogens, mutagens and free-radicals associated with diseases like diabetes, arthritis, heart disease and cancer.[16]

VERY IMPORTANT CAUTION: Those with a particularly sensitive digestive system or Irritable Bowel Syndrome, Colitis, Ulcerative Colitis, Ileitis, Ulcers or Crohn's Disease should always use extreme caution with *any* increase in raw veggies. For some, among other things a significant decrease in stomach flora balance has caused a significant lack of hydrochloric acid, causing difficulty in digesting many things – including raw veggies. In such cases it may be necessary to have a week or two of all cooked foods while supplementing with probiotics until the colon is re-lined again, healthy and able to better digest. There's more on this in my book 'The Biology of Beating Stress'. Always consult with your doctor before making any changes to your regimen.

*H*ow Many Times Should I Eat During My Day?

Honestly, having several (4-6) small meals / snacks (which always include protein) has been proven as the best method for maintaining healthy insulin levels. *Why is that important?* Because, this keeps your metabolism elevated and provides your body with a steady stream of nutrients (including amino acids from protein-containing foods).

You need to be very aware of your overall food consumption for the day and not let those calories get away from you ~ instead divide them. Keep in mind that, your breakfast shouldn't be so heavy that you can't eat a handful of raw nuts a few of hours later. Your meals should be small. The goal is to space your calories out so that you're never loading-in too much at one meal and your body is just ready to have something else by the time you get to your next one.

Yes, it can feel like you're eating all the time for some people and it does require some thought and preparation in terms of having yummy, healthy foods on hand that are also easy and simple to carry. But it's well worth it. Here are some other basic guidelines for you to consider:

Decrease (*or ideally eliminate*) your intake of:

- All processed or junk foods.
    - Foods containing refined white flour and sugar, such as breads, cereals (cornflakes, Frosted Flakes, puffed wheat and sweetened granola), flour-based pastas, bagels and pastries.
- All foods containing high-fructose corn syrup. Read Food Labels carefully.
- All artificial sweeteners (aspartame, sorbitol, splenda, truvia, etc.) and caffeine
- Starchy, high-glycemic cooked vegetables, such as potatoes, corn and root vegetables such as rutabagas, parsnips and turnips.
- Processed fruit juices, which are often loaded with sugars (Try juicing your own carrots, celery and beets or other fruit and vegetable combinations, instead).
- Processed canned vegetables (usually very high in sodium and at risk for BPA). Buy fresh organic produce.

- Foods containing hydrogenated or partially hydrogenated oils (which become trans fatty acids in the bloodstream), such as most crackers, chips, cakes, candies, cookies, doughnuts and processed cheese. Read Food Labels carefully.

- Processed oils such as corn, safflower, sunflower, peanut & canola – use coconut oil, red palm oil or rice bran oil instead.

- Red meats and organ meats. (unless organic or grass-fed) Protein from animal sources need not be eaten EVERY DAY! Once or twice a week is sufficient.

Our society, along with portion sizes also has a misconception about meal composition. Each person's required protein intake will vary. *Why?* It depends on sex, height, weight and exercise levels. Normal protein intake ranges from 20 to 50 grams each meal. Women are typically deficient in protein consumption. Generally, a 45-year-old woman needs 2 to 3 ounces of protein per meal, depending upon activity level. That's equivalent to ½ of a small chicken breast and a ½cup of cooked black beans – Yep, *Our portion sizes are out of control!*

High-protein diets, such as the Atkins diet, may actually accelerate kidney disease in people at risk. Since proteins must be broken down into amino acids in the body, and waste products excreted, too much protein puts a strain on the body's ability to get rid of waste products, especially in those who already have a kidney problem. Calcium loss, which leads to osteoporosis, also occurs with high levels of protein intake.

- Large predatory fish and river fish, which contain mercury and other contaminants in unacceptable amounts, including bass, perch, swordfish, tuna, tilefish and shark. *(Go with Wild Salmon, Cod, Sable, Sardines or Halibut instead)*

- Dairy -- substitute unsweetened, gluten free Hemp milk, almond milk or hazelnut milk products.

- Alcohol -- limit to no more than 3 glasses red wine per week.

You'll find much more about foods and health in my book 'The Biology of Beating Stress.'

So now that we've agreed that you're going to start a Food Diary….

○ Pay attention to your hunger level

○ Pause and savor your food as you eat (Don't talk on the phone or work at your desk while you eat ~ try to clear your mind ~ *ok* for your digestion's sake if not for your own enjoyment)

○ Stop when you feel comfortably full, not stuffed

○ Pay attention to the types of food you're drawn to (this will also 'clue you in' to whether this is possibly emotional eating rather than physical hunger

Here are some bodily sensations which you'll want to keep track of after eating:

cramps, cough, phlegmy, fatigue, restlessness, shakiness, muscle weakness, poor concentration, scattered, restless, irritable, agitated, hyper, balanced, alert, good stamina, energized, comfortably full….and many others that you'll discover yourself.

Try to notice patterns ~ and food combinations that may be helpful or harmful.

*F*ood Diary

Meal	Time	Hunger Level	Location	Food	Observations mood - physical
pre-breakfast					
breakfast					
1st Protein snack					
lunch					
2nd protein snack					
dinner					
3rd protein snack					
other					

74

But Are there Any Foods that Reduce Stress?

I wish that I could say, 'Yes, here are the foods that will instantly reduce your stress and thereby improve your health.' But.....really we have to look more towards preventing stress rather than reducing it. Stress has the unfortunate consequence of reducing nutrient absorption in your intestines (long term stress, even more so).

That said ~ there **are** foods known to boost serotonin levels (your feel good neurotransmitters), as well as other foods that will help you to reduce levels of cortisol and adrenaline (hormones known to negatively affect the body over a period of time and lead to higher stress levels).

Since we know that stress can instantly disrupt your blood sugar level, as well as your immune system, it is easy to see why it's recommended to always support blood sugar consistency [ex. having 4-6 small meals per day]. Blood sugar consistency also means that you avoid concentrated or overtly sugary foods like fruit juice, dried fruit and all added-sugar foods. This also explains the constant recommendations you hear to consume whole, natural foods that are high in natural fiber and that also provide you with a small amount of protein. Keeping your blood sugar stabilized is one important way to help *prevent* stress.

Caffeine can be problematic. This is why it's always recommended that you try to avoid caffeine-containing foods like coffee, tea and soda.

Consider choosing fish over red meats, because they are so packed full of important B vitamins. Vitamin B12 is one of the important vitamins involved in your production of serotonin, (the 'feel good' neurotransmitter) and its deficiency can even lead to depression. So for instance having Salmon a fish high in Omega-3 fatty acids also happens to keep your stress hormones cortisol and adrenaline from peaking.

Tryptophan is a precursor to Serotonin (synthesized in drugs Paxil and other SSRI's). You might have heard about it in association with the heavy, sleepy felling some people have after a traditional Thanksgiving meal where turkey is served. Sorry folks but, the research is in ~ you can't blame the turkey ~ Nope. That after meal fatigue really is just the result of you overeating. *Why?* Tryptophan is found in a lot of other foods which you probably have in more moderate amounts all the time. For instance, not just Turkey but, actually ANY poultry (a 4-ounce portion of either chicken or turkey breast) provides 350 - 390mg. It's also found in Spirulina, Spinach, Water Cress, Pumpkin seeds per one-fourth cup, 110mgs, Chia Seeds, Cod per 4-ounce serving, 330mgs, Kidney beans, black beans and split peas each contain 180mgs per cup.

A big part of what Tryptophan does, is assist the transmission of messages to and from your brain ~ kind of important all by itself, *Right?*

It's an essential amino acid and yes, a precursor of 5-HTP or serotonin. When it's converted by your body into serotonin it works with two other hormones, noradrenalin and dopamine, to lift your mood, promote relaxation and help deal with stress. But Tryptophan has other benefits. It combines with Vitamin B6, transforming into serotonin and niacin in your liver. This helps to improve not only your blood circulation, but also enhances memory and lower cholesterol, making tryptophan an essential amino acid to improve your overall health.

Want to know about a few other stress reducing foods?

You hear it all the time, 'Eat More Leafy Greens!' and so you should ~ Vegetables, especially dark green leafy vegetables are your healthy source of B vitamins. Consuming broccoli or asparagus both rich in folic acid, another B complex vitamin which is essential for your cell growth and reproduction also helps in the reduction of stress.

Vitamin B6 (pyridoxine, pyridoxal, pyridoxamine) is a water soluble vitamin and your body uses it for proper maintenance of your red blood cell metabolism, nervous system, immune system, and many other of your bodily functions. Over time, a deficiency in Vitamin B6 can lead to depression, confusion, convulsions, and even anemia. You can find it in natural sources like: Pistachio Nuts Per cup (123g)69% Daily Value; Sunflower Seeds Per cup (140g) 94% DV; Dried Prunes Per cup (132g) 49% DV; Cold water Fish & organic free-range Poultry - 3oz, cooked; Wild Salmon (40%), Halibut (27%) Herring (22%) Ground Turkey, Fat-free (46%), Chicken Breast (28%) and Chicken Wing (26%).

NuDay Perspectives Book

Kale, Swiss chard and spinach are all rich in folic acid they also contain calcium which is also known to have a calming effect. Dark leafy greens are known as a great source of calcium raw or cooked. Raw turnip greens provide the most calcium with 190mg (19% Daily Value) per 100 gram serving, or 105mg (10% DV) in a chopped cup. It is followed by Dandelion greens which provide 103mg (10%DV) per cup, Kale 9% DV per cup, Mustard Greens 6% DV per cup, and Collard greens 5% DV, Kelp has 168mg (17% DV) per 100 gram serving.

Stress can lead to a dramatic increase in free radicals as well as, damaging cortisol levels we talked about which will speed up the aging process and increase your disease risk. *Not Good.* Vitamin C you probably already think of as important for boosting your immune system *however,* a German study published in Psychopharmacology also found that Vitamin C helps to reduce stress and return blood pressure and cortisol to normal levels after a stressful situation.[7] Dr. Stuart Brody led a team based at the University of Trier in Germany, which studied 120 patients, half of whom received 1000mg of Vitamin C in three sustained-release pills [from GlaxoSmithBeecham, who funded the study]. Controls received placebo and were subjected to the same tests.

Dr. Brody told Reuters Health that "the subjects were asked every 10 minutes how they rated their stress levels on a scale of 1 to 10. This continued even after the induced stress, for *40 minutes afterwards.*" Also measured during the study were "objective measurements of stress", meaning things like systolic blood pressure and levels of cortisol, the stress hormone." The Trier Social Stress Test (which includes time honored stressors like - mathematic tasks and public speaking), was used to induce stress, Dr. Brody explained.

So, every day over a 2 week period the tests were conducted. Consistently, those taking Vitamin C handled their stress better. On top of that, the average increase in blood pressure was 31 mm Hg among the placebo subjects compared with 23 mm Hg for those who taking Vitamin C. *AND* the return to normal blood pressure and cortisol levels was also faster for the test subjects than for those who didn't have it. Dr. Brody also added that people felt less stressed when they were saturated with Vitamin C. "This kind of high dose of Vitamin C improves stress management," he stated.

"And I would say that it should be considered as part of an approach to dealing with stress."

So, those lovely dark leafy greens are more than just a source of calcium, they're packed with other vitamins including ~ you guessed it ~ Vitamin C. Raw kale provides the most Vitamin C with 120mg (200% DV) per 100 gram serving, 80mg (134% DV) per cup chopped. It is followed by mustard greens which provide 70mg (117% DV) per 100 gram serving, Broccoli provides 89mg (149% DV) of vitamin C in a 100g serving, 81mg (135% DV) per cup chopped, 28mg (46% DV) per piece. Raw cauliflower provides much less with 46mg (77% DV) per cup, raw Brussels sprouts provide 75mg (125% DV) per cup, 16mg (27% DV). These forms may be preferable to fruits like oranges which also have high sugar content.

Have you heard of Gamma-Aminobutyric Acid (or GABA for short)? *No?* Well, GABA slows anxiety (something like the synthetic drugs xanex or Valium) and your body actually makes this calming neurotransmitter naturally.

When you don't have adequate GABA and serotonin levels ~ not only will your worrying thoughts persist longer than they need to; *but* as they go around and around they can escalate, gain momentum and grow into enormous, unwieldy, disturbing levels of fear, stress and anxiety. Lions & Tigers and Bears ~ *Oh, My!*

Food to the rescue! You can find it naturally in fermented foods like Kefir, Kimchi or Sauerkraut.

When you think of Magnesium do you think of blood pressure lowering? How about sleep improvement? *You will now!* Magnesium is a powerhouse! It's an essential mineral required by your body in order to maintain normal muscle and nerve function, keep a healthy immune system, maintain heart rhythm, and build strong bones. Magnesium is also involved in at least 300 biochemical reactions in your body. In fact, magnesium deficiency can lead to muscle spasms, cardiovascular disease, diabetes, high blood pressure, anxiety disorders, migraines, osteoporosis and cerebral infarction.

In terms of relieving stress, the much needed sleep regulating hormone melatonin becomes limited whenever you're lacking in magnesium. It's also needed to for the balance and controls of stress hormones. Not to mention that our friend Serotonin, which relaxes the nervous system and elevates mood, is dependent on (*wait for it*) Magnesium.

Foods can naturally help you boost this all important nutrient. Nori; Quinoa per cup(195g) cooked 30% Daily Value; a variety of Nuts per 1/2 cup (113g) = Pumpkin Seeds (152% DV) Sesame Seeds (63%), Brazil Nuts (63%), Almonds (48%), Cashews (44% DV), Pine nuts (43%), Pecans (17%), Walnuts (16%).

Also, Squash per oz (28g) 150mg (37% DV); Lentils 1 Cup Cooked (172g) 148mg, 37% DV; White Beans 28% per cup cooked; Brown Rice 1 Cup Cooked (195g) 86mg 21% DV

Avocado is a great source of mono-unsaturated fat, making them a healthier option when stress leaves you craving high-fat foods. It is nutrient rich having nearly 20 vitamins and minerals including potassium, which helps lower blood pressure.

Almonds are rich in Vitamin E, another antioxidant that fights off the damaging free radicals that stress creates. They're also a good source of vitamin B2 and E, as well as magnesium and zinc, almonds are high in fat, but most of the fat is unsaturated. Like Vitamin C, Vitamin E has been shown to fight the free radicals associated with stress, and in particular, those free radicals that cause heart disease.

Complex carbohydrates increase your levels of serotonin, that mood-boosting neurotransmitter we talked about earlier. This includes foods hearty like amaranth, quinoa, oatmeal, lentils, kidney beans, black beans, peas, garbanzo beans and pinto beans. It also includes vegetables ~ Broccoli, cauliflower, spinach, turnip greens, eggplant, potatoes, yams, corn, carrots, onions, all types of lettuce, celery, cucumbers, cabbage, artichokes and asparagus.

In fact, yams and sweet potatoes can be particularly stress-reducing because they can satisfy the strong urge you get for carbohydrates and sweets when you are under a great deal of stress. They have fiber that helps your body to process carbohydrates in a slow and steady manner with a lower Glycemic index than that of a white potato. They have 380 percent of the recommended daily value of vitamin A, 35 percent of Vitamin C and are full of beta-carotene. Of course that's without butter or added sugar which can load on the pounds.

When you eat a healthy balanced diet which lowers your blood pressure and boosts your immune system, you are ultimately leading to lower your stress level too ~ and that's our goal!

*M*editation (or mini-vacation)

*M*aybe you've had an intention to mediate but, just can't seem to 'get around to it'; you used to meditate but, quit; or simply never learned how.

Here's the thing ~ training your body on a daily basis to achieve this state of relaxation can lead to enhanced mood, lower your blood pressure, improve your cardiovascular health, help you achieve a greater capacity for relaxation and decrease your compounded load of lifestyle stress. Meditation naturally restores your body to a calm state, helping it to repair itself and preventing new damage due to the physical effects of stress. It also will have you back to your old adorable self ~ or bring you to your new adorable self because it's known to relieve both anxiety and depression.

Yes, in as little as 5 – 20 minutes daily you (yes YOU!) can improve your health and over-all sense of well-being. Maybe this sounds like a late-night infomercial but, it's true!

When you practice meditation, your heart rate and breathing slow, your blood pressure normalizes and you use oxygen more efficiently. Because your adrenal glands produce less cortisol, your mind actually 'ages' at a slower rate and your immune function improves. Your memory actually improves, as well and your creativity is enhanced.

Just 5 – 20mins daily ~ this relatively small investment of time can amass HUGE benefits. All of this ~ and it's FREE! It's always available and has no potential side effects. And again ~ it's *FREE!* (Batteries not included)

If you're waiting for the 'downside' there is none. Some will say 'I just can't quiet my mind' or 'I don't know how to do it right'. Actually, here's a secret ~ you can't do it wrong. In whatever way you chose to meditate ~ for whatever time you allow ~ there is always some benefit. Always. Just the act of sitting and consciously intending relaxation, whether you are able to immediately register an improvement yourself ~ research has shown that there is an affect.

This is such an instant way to slow-down your life for just a few minutes and bring back a little sanity. This really is the very definition of 'Being' more. If I've made it sound incredibly easy do to ~ that's because it is. You'll find that once you take that 'giant leap' of committing 'x' amount of time to yourself ~ the rest is simple.

In this state of meditation, you are completely in the present moment and only that moment. We all seek clarity. What better way than to turn down the volume of thoughts, worries, concerns, hopes, prospects ~ so that you can actually think?

Do this for yourself in pockets of time; as much as you feel comfortable with, as often as you can. Hopefully, twice a day you'll find the time to meditate (or have a mini-vacation).

There is a lot more information on this in my book 'The Biology of Beating Stress'.

So let's get to it. I've got a couple of really simple but, enormously effective techniques for you to use......
Loosen your clothing, take off your shoes and get comfy.

*E*asy Meditation Technique:

A quiet space or out in nature would be nice, ideal in fact, but many of us simply don't have that luxury. That's Ok ~ anywhere will do. We're about to find the quiet space within YOU ~ the 'space between thoughts' as they say. So, just start wherever you are.

Now, find yourself a comfortable seating position.

You can use the floor or a chair (with a back).

Have your spine straight and not slouching. If in a chair, have both feet on the ground, shoulder width apart.

Sitting on the floor? Sit legs akimbo ~ in a cross-legged position.

Just be comfortable. Let anticipation and expectation go. Relax. This is easy.

☞ Close your eyes and breathe as naturally as possible. After a few breaths, try breathing more deeply with your abdomen only (you learned this earlier in the deep breathing exercise). Feel the belly rise and the slight movement in the ribcage, collarbones and shoulders as the breath moves upward. Slowly, your breath will naturally deepen as you practice. Focus on the sensation of the movement of air in and out of your nostrils.

Try inhaling to a count 5 - and exhaling likewise.

☞ Begin to quiet your mind. Of course, any sounds around you will be elevated ~ just hear them and let them go. Thoughts will come ~ don't struggle against them. Let the thoughts come, but don't dwell on them. Keep relaxing and bring your consciousness back to your breath.

If you have any trouble letting go, focus on just one thing∞

▶ A word or mantra can invoke a calming effect within you ~ for instance 'Aum', 'Om' or 'I Am'.

▶ Imagine an orb of brilliant, diamond-like white light just a foot above your head and feel it radiating down through every aspect of your being and surrounding you with healing and peace.

▶ Some find focusing on a sense of gratitude brings feelings of amazing contentment and Joy.

▶ Fill your heart with loving warmth and simply sit with that feeling as it radiates through and around you.

*M*editation Using Visualization

*T*his simple meditation easily helps you reduce tension and stress.

The Step by Step:

☞ Sit comfortably, close your eyes. Simply direct your attention to your breathing, just like you did in the first exercise.

☞ Be aware of every breath ~ both in and out. Observe, don't direct, as the air slowly glides in through your nose, fills up your lungs, and goes out again.

☞ Feel your body and mind begin to still themselves.

☞ With every breath, you start to feel the positive energy into your lungs.

☞ When you breathe out ~ imagine all negative feelings release from your body together with your breath.

☞ When you are totally relaxed, choose an image, a situation or an environment that represents 'rest', peace and calmness to you.

☞ Move around (in your imagination) and enjoy every moment in your favorite surroundings.

Involve all of your senses. Smell, taste, look and feel as many details as possible. Feel the sensations in your body, feel your muscles relaxing and notice your body reacting directly to everything that you create with your mind. Enjoy this image in all its details and pay attention to all the emotions that accompany it.

For instance take this time to imagine your perfect beach moment. Feel each sensation of your experience (the sun, smell of the water, a slight cooling breeze, the sound of the waves gently lapping). Really, really 'Be' there.

Actually, you can use any image you like: Splash through Buckingham Fountain in Chicago (feel the silliness) or fly like a Condor over the Grand Canyon (feel the freedom); blaze up the Pacific Coast Highway or Route 66 with the top down (feel the exhilaration); imagine money just pouring into your bank account and feel the delight of this wealth; visit with a departed loved one and really feel pleasure in their presence, enjoy a long missed game of tag with a childhood friend – *laugh!*

This is your time for yourself ~ *Your* moment. No one need know where you go or what you do. The only two rules are that you feel each sensation of your experience and you enjoy the heck out of it and also find a sense of astonishing Peace.

☛ Focus on this image and hold it in your mind as firmly as possible. Continue this visualization for as long as you like.

☛ Any time you are ready to stop, simply take your attention back to the rest of your body and become aware of yourself being in the room.

☛ Open your eyes.

Places to Go During My Visualization:

Kirtan Kriya

Sounds exotic doesn't it? However, a recent study at the Alzheimer's Research and Prevention Foundation in Arizona [published July 2012] showed that Kirtan Kriya can increase blood flow to the brain and improve memory, after just eight weeks practice. *Have I got your attention now?*

My goal was to find things for you which could be done within limited time, were simple - yet produced maximum benefit. This little gem is a good example.

So, can you find 12 minutes to spare each day? This is a very simple meditation chant exercise which originates from a form of yoga called Kundalini. Kirtan Kriya involves chanting and using finger poses - known as 'mudras'. It's thought that the 'mudras' reduce stress levels, increase blood circulation in the brain, promote focus and clarity and stimulate the mind-body-spirit connection.

The Step by Step:

Sit in a comfortable upright position with your back straight and supported. Relax.

Rest your hands on your upper thighs, palms facing upwards. Now focus your attention on the center of your forehead.

Chant the syllables: Sa, Ta, Na, Ma - so that the 'a' is the short vowel sound 'ah'.

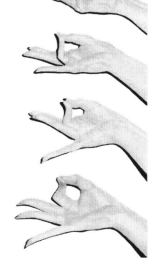

As you chant each syllable perform the following finger movements (Mudras):

- As you say 'Sa', press your index finger tip to the tip of your thumb
- As you say 'Ta' press your middle finger tip to the tip of your thumb.
- As you say 'Na' press your ring finger tip to the tip of your thumb.
- As you say 'Ma' press your pinky tip to the tip of your thumb.

Note: Please be mindful that you press your fingers firmly enough to be aware of the pressure and keep your attention focused but, don't pinch.

Say the chants use finger movements in this sequence:
- Chant out loud for 2 minutes
- Chant in a whisper for 2 minutes
- Chant in silence for 4 minutes
- Chant in a whisper for 2 minutes
- Chant out loud for 2 minutes

Visualize or feel each individual sound as a line of energy coming in through the top of your head [crown chakra], down through the middle of your head and out to infinity through the center of your forehead [third eye].

When you have finished this sequence, close your eyes; raise your arms overhead while inhaling and then exhale as your arms circle back down coming back to a resting position with your hands resting again on your thighs. Keep your eyes closed, breathing regularly until your attention comes back to your surroundings. Gently open your eyes.

You can also use Kirtan Kriya with your eyes closed using a very quiet timer set to go off every 2 minutes.

While doing this meditation, you may experience memories from your past, playing like a movie across the screen of your mind. Let them dance for a moment in front of your eyes and then release them with the mantra. You are just doing a little housekeeping in your unconscious mind.

If emotions come up, don't hold back - incorporate them into your chanting, i.e. if you feel anger then chant out the anger.

Whatever you experience is OK. Do not try to avoid or control your experience. Simply witness what's going on ~ and allow it. It is all part of your cleansing process.

*W*hy Sa, Ta, Na, Ma?

*K*undalini Yoga teachers use two principal mantras; SAT NAM and its derivative SA TA NA MA. Both are thought to represent the basic primal sounds that connect us (our souls) to the Universe. Sanskrit chanting sounds *Sa Ta Na Ma* translate to birth, life, death and rebirth. Through repetition of these sounds it is believed that we can 'rearrange' and rebalance our unconscious mind.

*S*leep

All of us know what it's like to go without enough sleep. It affects not only stress levels but, mood and efficiency. Getting adequate sleep is absolutely crucial to maintaining proper brain function ~ no less so than air, water and food ~ but, stress can easily disrupt sleep-wake cycles ~ to your detriment.
Here's what good consistent sleep does for you:

- Improves mood, including depression or anxiety.

- Helps your immune system mend your body at a cellular level when you are stressed or have been exposed to compromising elements, such as pollutants and infectious bacteria.

- Reduces levels of stress and inflammation in your body.

- Helps to keep blood pressure and cholesterol levels (which play a role in heart disease) in check.

- Improves cell degradation which if left un-checked propels aging.

- Increases focus and memory.

- Supports normal hormone balances which, among other things, stabilizes your appetite.

- Maximizes your body's ability to processes glucose (the carbohydrate your cells use for fuel) thereby reducing your risk for type-2 Diabetes.

All of these are covered in far more detail in my book, 'The Biology of Beating Stress'. However, here we will just focus on getting you 'some shut-eye.'

Just how much sleep is enough? Let's cite the experts. The National Institute of Neurological Disorders and Stroke reports that most adults need seven to eight hours of sleep nightly.
Are you getting optimal sleep?

Sleep Requirements by Age		
Newborns	(0-2 months old)	12-18 hours
Infants	(3-11 months old)	14-15 Hours
Toddlers	(1-3 years old)	12-14 Hours
Pre-schoolers	(3-5 years old)	11-13 Hours
School-aged Children	(5-10 years old)	10-11 Hours
Teens	(11-17 years old)	8-9 Hours
Adults		7-9 Hours

Research shows that people who do get the appropriate amount of sleep on a regular basis tend to actually live longer, healthier lives than those who sleep too few or even too many hours each night.[8]

The benefits of sleep are extensive and will make a real difference in your quality of life, as well as the length of your life. It's vital to place a priority on getting ample, consistent, quality sleep.

So let's look into some helpful tools to help you get enough zzzzzzzzzzzz's

*B*ody Scan

*A*s mentioned when we discussed stretching ~ all of us become so accustomed to holding onto tension. In fact, we become unaware of body positions and even body parts which are holding onto our tension. *Yep!* Tension becomes the norm!

Here's an easy way to begin to break this vicious cycle......

- Lie comfortably on your back, eyes open or closed, arms relaxed at your sides, hands flat, legs uncrossed. Bring your awareness to your breathing, allowing your stomach to rise as you inhale and fall as you exhale. Breathe deeply for about two minutes, until you start to feel more calm and relaxed.

- Turn your awareness to the toes of your right foot. Notice any sensations there while continuing to also be mildly aware of your breathing. Imagine each deep breath flowing gently into your toes. Remain with this for one or two minutes.

- Move your awareness to the sole of your right foot. Tune-in to any sensations you feel there and imagine each breath flowing into the sole of this foot. After one or two minutes, move your awareness to your right ankle and repeat this. Move upwards to your calf, knee, thigh and hip.

- Repeat this same sequence for your left leg.

- Now, move up your torso, through the lower back and abdomen, your upper back and chest, and across your shoulders. Pay close attention to any area of the body that causes you pain or discomfort. Breathe release into these and relax.

- Move your awareness towards the fingers on your right hand and move upwards to your wrist, forearm, elbow, upper arm and shoulder.

- Repeat for your left arm.

- Move your awareness across your neck and throat and finally all the regions of your face, the back of the head, and the top of the head. Pay close attention to your jaw, chin, lips, tongue, nose, cheeks, eyes, forehead, temples and scalp.

- When you have reached the very top of your head ~ let your breath reach out beyond your body and imagine that you are hovering above yourself. Enjoy this sensation of lightness and freedom.

- After completing your body scan, relax for a while in silence and stillness, noting how your body feels.

- Then open your eyes slowly. Take a moment to stretch.

*A*ttention List

Before you go to bed hand write out any lingering thoughts *at all* ('to-do' lists, conversations left incomplete or which need happen, memories that loop). Hand write them all into list form on a sheet of paper with the intent and knowledge that they will be addressed the following day but, for now must be put away to allow your mind and body the precious time it needs to relax and re-vitalize.

This really very simple tool puts your unconscious mind more at ease, because you have consciously acknowledged those lose threads. Writing them by hand is an important part of this.

Be certain to list also a few of the things that you accomplished that are positive during your day – it's important to also recognize achievements and we sometimes forget to give ourselves a much needed pat on the back.

You'll be amazed at how this simple little tool can transform your life. When you review these lists from time to time - you'll begin to notice patterns that creep-up in your life – repeated issues that you can now see clearly need some attention – *just not when you're about to go to sleep!*

My Attention List for the Night:
Date_____

1. _____
Solutions/Follow-up:

2. _____
Solutions/Follow-up:

3. _____
Solutions/Follow-up:

4. _____
Solutions/Follow-up:

5. _____
Solutions/Follow-up:

*L*iberation Word

*S*o you're lying there - things going back and forth in your mind. You check the clock counting down to wake-up time. The thoughts keep coming. Believe it or not this is a remnant of your speech center development which starts at about 3 months old. You've seen babies randomly cooing, gurgling and making otherwise unintelligible sounds which their parents will swear that they understand. Your speech center 'practices' sounds repetitively as you develop language skills. But in this instance your subconscious anxieties and stress have co-opted this little skill. Well, here's a great trick to reclaim your head space.

As soon as you realize that you're 'thought rambling' – and sometimes it may take a while to even recognize this ~ use the liberation word that you've selected. (Mine is 'Zucchini' for no particular reason other than I liked the sound of it.) Begin repeating your liberation word quietly in your head. Free your mind! It will gradually displace or crowd-out your rambling thoughts and you'll begin to drift back to sleep.

In a similar way to the brainwave entrainment we discussed earlier, as you use this tool more and more, less repetitions of your liberation word will be necessary to carry you back into peaceful slumber.

Sleep Hygiene

We must all take a little "holiday" in the 2 hours before bed. **You must train yourself to relax -** even if you have to patiently coerce it by laying in the dark and consciously, gently relaxing each body part and emptying your mind – several times - to truly unwind. Use these simple tips to get between 7 and 9 hours of sleep, which can have dramatic positive effects on your *health:*

- Avoid any stimulating activities for 2 hours before bed such as watching TV, using the Internet and answering emails.

- Create a Sleep Ritual – Yep! It sounds corny but, a special set of little things you do before bed to help ready your system physically and psychologically for sleep – can guide your body into a deep, healing sleep.

- Exercise daily for 20 minutes (but not 3 hours before bed, which can affect sleep)

- Avoid substances that affect sleep, like caffeine, sugar and alcohol.

- Practice the regular rhythms of sleep – go to bed and wake up at the same time each day. Try to go to bed preferably before 10 or 11 pm.

- Create an aesthetic environment that encourages sleep by using serene restful colors, eliminating clutter & distraction. Use your bed only for sleep and sexual activities.

- Don't eat or drink within 2 hours of bedtime.

- Hand write your Attention List

- Do Deep Breathing Exercises for at least 5 - 15mins just before you get into bed.

- Put-on eye ware to block out blue light 2- 3 hours prior to bedtime; even better right after sunset.

- Get a massage OR do some gentle stretching

- Take a warm salt/soda aromatherapy bath. Raising your body temperature before bed helps to induce sleep. A warm bath also relaxes your muscles and reduces tension physically and psychologically.

By adding ½ to 1 cup of Epsom Salt (magnesium sulfate) and ½ to 1 cup of baking soda (sodium bicarbonate) to your bath, you will gain the benefits of magnesium absorbed through your skin and the alkaline-balancing effects of the baking soda, both of which aid sleep.

You might even add and 10 drops of lavender essential oil to your bathwater.

- Keep your bedroom very dark or use eyeshades.

- Block out sound if you have a noisy environment by using earplugs (soft silicone ones work well).

- Make the room a comfortable temperature for sleep – not too hot or cold.

Nutritional Compliments to Consider for Sleep

- Consider relaxing minerals such as Magnesium citrate or glycinate before bed (which relaxes the nervous system and muscles). It is best to take Magnesium with Calcium (at a 1:1 ratio 500mgs).

- Herbal Remedies: Consider Passion Flower or Valerian (valeriana officinalis) root extract standardized to 0.2 percent valerenic acid, Chamomile, Holy Basil, Wild Lettuce Leaf extract, Suma, Skullcap, Ashwagandha or Lemon Balm one hour before bed. Other supplements and herbs can be helpful in getting some shut-eye, such as L-Theanine (an amino acid from green tea), Glycine Powder, GABA, 5-HTP and Magnolia. Experiment with herbal combinations or blends to find the best effect for you.

- Melatonin supplementation is a popular choice.

Always check with your doctor before beginning any new health regimen or supplement.

*B*rain Wave Entrainment

*S*imply put ~ for you to get to sleep, your brainwave frequency (which is based on your brain's activity level) needs to drop to a nice slow Delta wave from the heightened Beta state that it uses when you're alert. At times, this can be challenging, especially on those hectic days. Your brain can stay active when you've had a busy day which can then keep you from getting the nourishing sleep that you really need. An effective way of inducing a change in your brainwave state is by using 'Binaural Beats.'

What are Binaural Beats? Binaural exactly means "having or relating to two ears." The sensation of 'auditory' binaural beats used in Brainwave Entrainment occur when two clear sounds (of nearly similar frequencies) are presented (one to each ear), through stereo headphones or speakers. So in a nutshell, you've got a different signal being broadcast to each ear which then create a third signal in the middle. This third sound is called the *binaural beat*. Binaural beats in fact originate naturally in your brain stem's superior olivary nucleus, the site of contra-lateral integration of auditory input.

While this may sound at first like something out of Science Fiction ~ it's true! Without medication or side effects this technique can relax most people within minutes. Brainwave entrainment through the use of binaural beats is a technique offering an easy and natural method to put your mind into a state of deep relaxation.

By using these Binaural Beats, you can quickly induce the frequencies associated with sleep into your brain, within minutes. *How?*

Researchers discovered that our brains will actually synchronize to the dominant frequency. Which means simply, that by inducing a new lower frequency (using binaural beats), your brain will begin naturally to lower its frequency to match that of the new frequency.

So ~ bottom-line, if an external stimulus (binaural beat broadcast through stereo headphones) is applied to the brain, it becomes possible to 'entrain' the brain frequency from one brain state to another.

For instance, let's say a person is in the Alpha state (highly alert) and a stimulus of 10Hz is applied to his/her brain for some time. Naturally, the brain frequency will make a gradual shift towards the applied stimulus. The person will experience a gradual relaxation. This phenomenon is the 'Frequency Following Response'.[9] Another means is through Isochronic Tones which uses equal intensity tones, but the pulse speed is greater, causing the brain to synchronize with the rhythm.

The next piece is the 'entrainment' piece. When a certain brainwave state is experienced and practiced over a period of time, your brain will "learn" the state change and it will become easier to self-produce that same desired brainwave state ~ at will. Also this means that, through using brainwave entrainment, it's possible to expect to get some of its effects later ~ even without any external stimulus. That's pretty amazing.

How does this cause 'The Relaxation Response'?

Your brain enters into a few different states during the day. Each of these states generates its own measureable and unique frequency. These are:

Beta (13 – 40 Hz)   Active, alert and focused
Alpha (8 -12 Hz)   Relaxed, calm and creative
Theta (4 – 8 Hz)   Drowsy, light sleep and dreams
Delta (less than 4 Hz) Deep sleep

Brainwave Entrainment, by broadcasting waves specifically in the Delta and Theta level range; will prompt your brain waves directly into a natural Relaxation Response.[10] This mental, physical and emotional state is characterized by lowered blood pressure decreased heart, breathing and metabolic rates and mind/body coherence ~ all good things.

Harvard professor Dr. Herbert Benson, founder of the Mind/Body Medical Institute at Boston's Deaconess Hospital, coined this term. Through research, he concluded that this Relaxation Response produces many long-term health benefits in addition to the immediate effects created during the Brainwave Entrainment experience. This is a dynamic way to trigger the natural healing mechanisms of your body!

Physically, the Relaxation Response:
- reduces oxygen consumption (hypometabolism)
- decreases blood pressure
- slows heart rate
- diminishes respiration rate
- relaxes muscles

Mentally, Deep Relaxation:
- changes brain wave frequencies (generally slowing from Beta to Theta/Delta)
- clears the mind from anxiety
- creates a feeling of calm and peacefulness

Isn't this cheating? YES – *well sort of.* We are so often challenged for time – a little nudge which is non-pharmacological and non-addictive related seems like an acceptable compromise. Brainwave Entrainment use can bring not only deep relaxation but, also enhanced meditation, reduction of insomnia and the symptoms of stress. Over time its effects can be sustained thereby allowing a person to basically re-learn how to relax on their own.

Much research has been done to advance the usage of Brainwave Entrainment and there's more info on it included in my book 'The Biology of Beating Stress'. You can also learn more at my website www.VibroAcousticsNY.com where you can even pick-up CD's or download tracks which employ them for use in relaxation, meditation and improved focus for studying.

It's another tool for you to consider in slowing down the flurry of life so that you can 'Be' more.

Release Your Smile

As mentioned in the book ~ At the very core, the essence of your being – you were designed for Joy. *Proof?* Every single living thing moves instinctively away from flames of fire knowing the pain and destruction it will bring. You too move intuitively away from that which brings pain and towards pleasure. Only when we're out of balance does this natural proclivity alter – like under STRESS!

Did you know that you already possess an amazingly powerful tool to relieve stress which is as close as your nose?.....Your Smile!

Get this – Just the simple the physical act of smiling actually produces an emotional effect and releases endorphins (which are natural pain relievers), along with serotonin, (which is also associated with feel good properties). If you try smiling, even when it's difficult to smile (like when you're not really feeling good); research shows that significant improvements can occur from this one tiny action. You've got absolutely nothing to lose and everything to gain.

So get out your pencil. *Why?*

Strange but true ~ holding a pen or pencil in your lips for just 60 seconds, has been shown to have a real effect on your emotional happiness levels!

Just hold a pencil or pen between your teeth (across from cheek to cheek, which naturally activates the muscles typically used for smiling)… *go on, try it now!!* As you can see and feel, this simple effort forces your mouth and face to smile, and yes ~ *Improves Mood!*

The expression "fake it 'til you make it," comes to mind and there's evidence that it is true! William Fleeson, an Associate Professor in Psychology and researcher in personality at Wake Forest University says, "Personality is often thought of as something you're born with it and it causes you to act a certain way. Theorists who approach personality from this structural perspective believe a person has a certain way of behaving, and although he or she may be able to override it on occasion, personality is part of nature. I'm not sure that's true. An alternative approach, one that

I'm interested in, suggests that personality is active and flexible."
To prove his point Fleeson conducted a study in which a group of
50 students were instructed to act like extroverts for 15 minutes in a
group discussion, even if they didn't feel like it. The findings? The
more assertive and energetic the students acted, the happier they
were".[11]

So let loose that smile ~ why not? In addition to actually improving
your mood it also:

- Lowers Blood Pressure

- Boosts Immune System actually stimulates immune
  response by helping you relax.

- It takes 17 muscles to smile and 43 to frown.

Conclusion

So now, as our little blue-green earth makes yet another swing around the sun at some ridiculous speed, let's take a moment and just notice how amazing you really are (yes, even as you just sit there reading). With over 7 billion human beings along for this ride, YOU remain singularly unique. Foibles and faults not withstanding you are still undeniably ~ amazing.

Don't be deceived by the flesh and blood density that makes-up your hardware ~ you are primarily a being of energy. Every one of your 1050 trillion cells is alive with it. Your body's own metabolism generates its very own electromagnetic field which can be measured and creates a faint bioluminescence (dim florescence) that can be captured by ultrasensitive equipment known as a cryogenic charge-coupled-device (CCD) camera. That's right – you glow! The amount of electricity your brain alone generates is roughly between 24 and 80 watts of power (more of it while you sleep by the way). Nerve impulses (to and from your brain) travel as fast as 170 miles per hour. It's difficult not to make an analogy to the computers we use. But, what's your operating system?

Animus, Essence, Spirit, Soul ~ whichever your tag, the only certainty about it is that it is your personalized, individual ticket to this astounding adventure.

The second certainty ~ change. As the earth makes its journey in space creating our sense of time, things will continue to change ~ you will continue to change during the time of your swing around the sun.

Our goal then ~ is to make your adventure a little smoother for you. Even with its ups and downs, (and you're guaranteed generous portions of each) ~ you can control a bit of your reaction to your experience. When you use the 'Stop Technique' to tune-in, when you use deep breathing, stretching and meditation to quell the fire and release some of your built-up tension ~ you're changing your response to whatever is happening in your life.

By reducing the pressures that you feel from stress you will be able to see things more clearly, take action with more clarity. You have to be present. You have to be aware of what's going on inside and out ~ you can only do this if you make a little room for it. Every day, capture just moments where you calm the constant outside noise and inner chatter. You will do it because you will immediately find that you no longer feel rushed and overwhelmed ~ you will reduce anxiety and stress.

You are so much more than the sum of your biochemical functions. Science, (including Schrodinger's Cat, Heisenberg's uncertainty principle, the double-slit experiment, nonlocal entanglement and quantum coherence) considers that your consciousness and specifically your conscious *observation* actually shapes the universe *as you perceive it*. Yep, they are close to saying we think our experience into being. They're still murky on the details of consciousness itself. They can't even define it (or locate its source within the brain or body). Yet, if you think about it for just a moment, taking into account that we've established already that we're really just energy ~ then where is 'in here' and 'out there'?

One thing is sure ~ your reaction, your perception, the way you internalize what happens in your experience, what you believe about what's happening ~ that is what makes the difference in the way that you feel, in the way that your body reacts and finally in interpreting what the experience you're having really *means*. This directly shapes your reality.

You do it all the time, but often you're doing so, without the benefit of a calm and focused mind. You're doing it under stress. You're perception is informed and warped by stress. Using the techniques we've covered in this book ~ you can begin to see things with more clarity and directly change your perception and thereby you will change your reality.

You know how you're sitting in a new restaurant waiting to order and you kind of eye the plates of other diners ~ to get an idea of what the food is going to be like (and maybe occasionally pass a little judgment also on whether or not that person might have been better-off ordering a small green salad instead of those fries). We fall into this same trap. We judge our experience based on that of those around us. This does not serve you well. *Why?*

You have no idea the journey that that person took to arrive where they are. Maybe that's his last big meal before he's going away to a weight-loss program. Maybe the salmon on the other person's plate is excellent, but by the time you order the same dish, that chef has suddenly left the restaurant with a bad case of stomach flu and only the dish-washer 'Manny' is left to get the food out. But maybe this is Manny's big break and he's been studying at culinary school and so he's determined to 'rock the house' with his food and when your order arrives at *your* table, it is even more spectacular. You just never know.

Focus on *your* table. Pick from the menu the experiences that *you* want to have. Select options that have ingredients that you know will be healthiest for you; that are in-line with your needs or desires in this moment. Remember your guiding principles and be mindful of them as you make decisions. Be kind and gentle with yourself. Remind yourself of your strengths and find ways to work on any areas of concern. Your goals are not laws ~ they will change and you must allow for fluidity. Invite guests to your table who share common goals and interests. Keep your eyes and ears open for the next new experience, the next change ~ because there will always be something new on your horizon, but it doesn't have to be stressful*!* 'Be' More ~ Stress-less.

About the author:

Jeanne Ricks,CHC has a passion for teaching and sharing information about how we can all optimize our health and improve our sense of well-being.

As recent Director of Holistic Wellness Programs for City College of New York, she developed programs which emphasize self-healing through nutrition, breathing techniques and meditation; self-empowerment through practical techniques for coping with stress, building health and vitality, and developing inner resources to confront adversity and challenges in one's life.

Her outreach not only empowers the average person but, also reach those battling alcoholism, drug addiction, domestic violence, mental illness and the isolation often experienced by the elderly.

She is an independent nutritional consultant, lecturer, author and life coach whose motto is;
"As we instill new ideas – behavior changes – health improves.'

Other Books:
'The Biology of Beating Stress' ISBN:978-1-60163-330-9
New Page Books

Her websites are:

www.NuDay.org

www.VibroAcousticsNY.com

Notes:

1. Page 8 |P.M. Ridker, N. Rifai, L. Rose, J.E. Buring, and N.R. Cook, Comparison of C-Reactive Protein and Low-Density Lipoprotein Cholesterol Levels in the Prediction of First Cardiovascular Events, New England Journal of Medicine, November 14, 2002 Vol. 347 No. 20; 1557 - 1165

2. Page 41 |Andrej Stančák,Michal Kuna, "EEG changes during forced breathing", International Journal of Psychophysiology [Elsevier], October 1994

3. Page 41   Jella SA1, Shannahoff-Khalsa DS; 'The effects of unilateral forced nostril breathing on cognitive performance.'Int J Neurosci. 1993 Nov;73(1-2):61-8.

4 . Page 45

Tovin, Brian J., Steven L. Wolf, Bruce H. Greenfield, Jeri Crouse, and Blane A. Woodfin. "Comparison of the effects of exercise in water and on land on the rehabilitation of patients with intra-articular anterior cruciate ligament reconstructions." Physical Therapy 74, no. 8 (1994): 710-719

5. Page 55 |Sevits, Kyle; Peltonen, Garrett; et al. "abstract of the study entitled, "A Single Session of Sprint Interval Training Increases Total Daily Energy Expenditure." Today@Colorado State; Colorado State University October 16, 2012

6. Page 60 |Peterson, Mark D.; Gordon, Paul M., "Resistance Exercise for the Aging Adult: Clinical Implications and Prescription Guidelines." The American Journal of Medicine, 2011; 124 (3): 194 DOI: 10.1016/j.amjmed.2010.08.020

7. Page 76 -77 |Brody, Stuart, Ragnar Preut, Kerstin Schommer, and Thomas H. Schürmeyer. "A randomized controlled trial of high dose ascorbic acid for reduction of blood pressure, cortisol, and subjective responses to psychological stress." Psychopharmacology 159, no. 3 (2002): 319-324.

8. Page 92 |Cappuccio FP; D'Elia L; Strazzullo P; Miller MA. Sleep duration and all-cause mortality: a systematic review and meta-analysis of prospective studies. SLEEP 2010;33(5):585-592

9. Page 101 |Smith, James C., James T. Marsh, and Warren S. Brown. "Far-field recorded frequency-following responses: evidence for the locus of brainstem sources." Electroencephalography and clinical neurophysiology 39, no. 5 (1975): 465-472.

10. Herbert Benson, M. D., and Miriam Z. Klipper. 'The Relaxation Response'. Harper Collins, New York, 1992.

11. Page 106 |Fleeson, William, Adriane B. Malanos, and Noelle M. Achille. "An intraindividual process approach to the relationship between extraversion and positive affect: is acting extraverted as" good" as being extraverted?." Journal of personality and social psychology 83, no. 6 (2002): 1409.

12. Page 51 |Janice K. Kiecolt-Glaser, Ph.D., Lisa Christian, Ph.D., et al.; 'Stress, Inflammation and Yoga Practice'; Psychosom Med. Feb 2010; 72(2): 113. PMC2820143

13. Page 51 |Innes, Kim E. ; Selfe, Terry Kit , 'The Effects of a Gentle Yoga Program on Sleep, Mood, and Blood Pressure in Older Women with Restless Legs Syndrome (RLS): A Preliminary Randomized Controlled Trial', Published online Feb 28, 2012. doi: 10.1155/2012/294058 PMCID: PMC3303621

14. Page 69 | Sequin, Rebecca A., Jacqueline N. Epping, David M. Buchner, Rina Bloch, and Miriam E. Nelson. "Growing stronger: strength training for older adults." (2002).

15. Page 69 | Paddon-Jones, D., Symons, T. Brock, et al. "A moderate serving of high-quality protein maximally stimulates skeletal muscle protein synthesis in young and elderly subjects." Journal of the American Dietetic Association 109.9 (2009): 1582-1586.

16. Page 69 |McGee, Harold. On food and cooking: the science and lore of the kitchen. Simon and Schuster, 2007. Vyas, Bharti, Le Quesne, Suzanne. 'The pH Balance Diet: Restore Your Acid-Alkaline Levels to Eliminate Toxins and Lose Weight' Ulysses Press; 1 edition 6 July 2007

114

References:

"Essentials of Strength Training and Conditioning"; Thomas R. Baechle, et al.; 2000

"American Journal of Sports Medicine"; Muscle Flexibility as a Risk Factor for Seveloping Muscle Injuries . . .; Erik Witvrouw, et al.; January-February 2003

The Stretching Institute: PNF Stretching Explained -- Proprioceptive Neuromuscular Faciliation; Brad Walker; 2011

Astin JA, Shapiro SL, Eisenberg DM, Forys KL. Mind-Body Medicine: State of the Science, Implications for Practice. The Journal of the American Board of Family Practice March / April 2003. Bonadonna, Ramita PhD. Meditation's Impact on Chronic Illness. Holistic Nursing Practice. November/December 2003.

Bowen S, Witkiewitz K, Dillworth TM, Chawla N, Simpson TL, Ostafin BD, Larimer ME, Blume AW, Parks GA, Marlatt GA. Mindfulness meditation and substance use in an incarcerated population. Psychology of Addictive Behaviors. September 20, 2006.

Chan, Cecilia, et al. The effect of a one-hour Eastern stress management session on salivary cortisol.Stress and Health. February 20, 2006.

Davidson, Richard, et. al. Alterations in Brain and Immune Function Produced by Mindfulness Meditation.Psychosomatic Medicine, 2003.

Pagnoni G, Cekic M. Age Effects on Gray Matter Volume and Attentional Performance in Zen meditation..Neurobiology of Aging. July 25, 2007.

Paul-Labrador M, Polk D, Dwyer JH, Velasquez I, Nidich S, Rainforth M, Schneider R, Merz CN. Effects of a Randomized Controlled Trial of Transcendental Meditation on Components of the Metabolic Syndrome in Subjects with Coronary Heart Disease.. Archives of Internal Medicine. June 12, 2006

Ekman, P. The Duchenne smile: Emotional experience and brain physiology: II. Journal of Personality and Social Psychology, 58, 342-353. (1990).

Kleinke, C. Influence of reinforced smiling on affective responses in an interview. Journal of Personality and Social Psychology, 42, 557-565. (1982).

Laird, J. Self-attribution of emotion: The effects of expressive behavior on the quality of emotional experience. Journal of Personality and Social Psychology, 29, 475-486. (1974).

Soussignan, R. Duchenne smile, emotional experience, and autonomic reactivity: A test of the facial feedback hypothesis. Journal of Personality and Social Psychology, 2, 52-74. Emotion, Vol 2(1), Mar 2002, 52-74. doi: 10.1037/1528-3542.2.1.52 (2002).

Fleeson, William; Malanos, Adriane B.; Achille, Noelle M. An intraindividual process approach to the relationship between extraversion and positive affect: Is acting extraverted as "good" as being extraverted? Journal of Personality and Social Psychology, Vol 83(6), Dec 2002, 1409-1422.

Kobayashi M, Kikuchi D, Okamura H (2009) Imaging of Ultraweak Spontaneous Photon Emission from Human Body Displaying Diurnal Rhythm. PLoS ONE 4(7): e6256. doi:10.1371/journal.pone.0006256

24930748R00070

Made in the USA
Middletown, DE
12 October 2015